Reading for Meaning

How to Build Students' Comprehension, Reasoning, and Problem-Solving Skills

A STRATEGIC TEACHER  GUIDE

Reading for Meaning

How to Build Students' Comprehension, Reasoning, and Problem-Solving Skills

Harvey F. Silver | Susan C. Morris | Victor Klein

ASCD

Alexandria, Virginia USA

A GUIDE FOR PROFESSIONAL LEARNING COMMUNITIES

1703 N. Beauregard St. • Alexandria, VA 22311-1714 USA
Phone: 800-933-2723 or 703-578-9600 • Fax: 703-575-5400
Web site: www.ascd.org • E-mail: member@ascd.org
Author guidelines: www.ascd.org/write

Gene R. Carter, *Executive Director;* Judy Zimny, *Chief Program Development Officer;* Nancy Modrak, *Publisher;* Scott Willis, *Director, Book Acquisitions & Development;* Carolyn Pool, *Acquisitions Editor;* Julie Houtz, *Director, Book Editing & Production;* Miriam Goldstein, *Editor;* Georgia Park, *Senior Graphic Designer;* Mike Kalyan, *Production Manager;* Keith Demmons, *Typesetter;* Kyle Steichen, *Production Specialist*

"Woggle" illustration on page 16
Released test item from the Connecticut Academic Performance Test: Second Generation Science Handbook (p. 38). © 2001 Connecticut Department of Education. Used with permission.

Image of etching on page 17
Image © The Metropolitan Museum of Art/Art Resource, New York
Goya y Lucientes, Francisco de (1746–1828). And There's Nothing to Be Done (Y no hai remedio). 1810–1820; published 1863. Etching, drypoint, burin, and burnisher, Sheet: 5 11/16 x 6 1/2 in. (14.5 x 16.51 cm). Harris Brisbane Dick Fund, 1932 (32.62.17).

Short story on pages 26–27
"A Nincompoop," from *Anton Chekhov: Selected Stories* by Anton Chekhov, translated by Ann Dunnigan, © 1960 by Ann Dunnigan. Used by permission of Dutton Signet, a division of Penguin Group (USA) Inc.

All web links in this book are correct as of the publication date below but may have become inactive or otherwise modified since that time. If you notice a deactivated or changed link, please e-mail books@ascd.org with the words "Link Update" in the subject line. In your message, please specify the web link, the book title, and the page number on which the link appears.

PAPERBACK ISBN: 978-1-4166-1132-5   ASCD product #110128   n12/10
Quantity discounts for the paperback edition only: 10–49 copies, 10%; 50+ copies, 15%; for 1,000 or more copies, call 800-933-2723, ext. 5634, or 703-575-5634. For desk copies: member@ascd.org.

Library of Congress Cataloging-in-Publication Data
Silver, Harvey F.
  Reading for meaning : how to build students' comprehension, reasoning, and problem-solving skills / Harvey F. Silver, Susan C. Morris, and Victor Klein.
      p. cm. -- (A strategic teacher PLC guide)
  Includes bibliographical references.
  ISBN 978-1-4166-1132-5 (pbk. : alk. paper) 1. Reading comprehension. 2. Reasoning--Study and teaching. 3. Problem solving--Study and teaching. I. Morris, Susan C. II. Klein, Victor. III. Title.
  LB1573.7.S58 2010
  372.41--dc22
                              2010035633

20 19 18 17 16 15 14 13 12 11 10   1 2 3 4 5 6 7 8 9 10 11 12

It is difficult to imagine this work having taken shape without the wisdom of our dear and deeply missed friend, Richard Strong. Richard's brilliant work in helping schools become better and more thoughtful places will continue to inspire us.

Reading for Meaning

How to Build Students' Comprehension, Reasoning, and Problem-Solving Skills

Acknowledgments

Action Research Team

Joyce Wagers Jackson
Daniel R. Moirao, EdD
Barb Heinzman

The work of these Thoughtful Classroom trainers and coaches in schools across the country played a critical role in the development of the Strategic Teacher PLC Guides. The feedback the team brought back from teachers, teacher leaders, and administrators made each successive version—and there were many versions—more powerful and more practical for educators.

Special thanks go to the Green River Regional Educational Cooperative (GRREC) in Kentucky, where earlier versions of these Strategic Teacher PLC Guides were piloted with more than 100 schools. It was the vision of teacher leadership shared by Liz Storey, Jamie Spugnardi, and hundreds of other teacher leaders and administrators from GRREC schools that helped us realize the potential of this new approach to building professional learning communities in schools.

Thank you to Matthew Perini for helping us give shape and polish to our ideas, and to Kristen Perini and Katarina Kokkosis for helping us think through the process of assessing student work.

To the wonderful staff at ASCD—Nancy Modrak, Ann Cunningham-Morris, Julie Houtz, Jean Pride, Debbie Brown, Genny Ostertag, Miriam Goldstein, and many others—thank you for your support and enthusiasm for these new products we call Strategic Teacher PLC Guides. But the greatest debt of thanks goes to Scott Willis. Without Scott's guidance and his ability to see the big picture and think through the details, we don't know where we'd be.

Finally, for never letting us—or our schools—forget the central role that thought plays in every act of teaching and learning, we would like to thank Art Costa and Bena Kallick. We are proud to integrate your work in building students' habits of mind into these Strategic Teacher PLC Guides.

Introduction

A New Professional Development Tool

You're holding a new kind of professional development tool called a Strategic Teacher PLC Guide. Designed in partnership with more than 75 schools, Strategic Teacher PLC Guides make the important work of bringing high-impact, research-based instructional practices into every classroom easier than ever before. Each guide focuses on one research-based strategy and serves as a complete professional development resource for a team of teachers to learn, plan, and implement the strategy in their classrooms.

This Strategic Teacher PLC Guide focuses on Reading for Meaning, a reading and reasoning strategy that helps students understand new ideas, make inferences, and support their thinking with evidence. The strategy is designed around findings from an extensive body of research showing that proficient readers outperform their less proficient peers for two main reasons. First, proficient readers use a specific set of thinking skills to build deep understanding of the texts they read. Second, proficient readers apply these skills in three distinct phases: before reading, during reading, and after reading. Reading for Meaning gives all students the opportunity to practice and master the skills and the three-phase approach of proficient readers by

- Using simple statements to preview and predict *before reading*.

- Actively searching for relevant evidence *during reading*.

- Reflecting on and synthesizing both their learning and their thinking process *after reading*.

The Reading for Meaning strategy also integrates the habits of mind, a set of dispositions that increase students' capacity for skillful thinking (Costa & Kallick, 2008, 2009).

Turning Knowledge into Practice

Here are three things we know about improving teaching and learning:

1. High-quality instruction leads invariably to higher levels of student achievement. Most educational researchers have concluded that the quality of classroom instruction is the single greatest determinant of student success.

2. High-quality instruction is replicable. There are specific, research-based strategies that are proven to raise student achievement—and that all teachers can master with time and support.

3. Schools that function as effective professional learning communities see "big, often immediate, dividends in student learning and professional morale in virtually any setting" (Schmoker, 2005, p. xii).

In other words, we know that we need to focus on improving instruction, we know which strategies will work, and we know that professional learning communities are key to any such efforts. But knowing these statements to be true doesn't mean that change is easy. In fact, we have worked with thousands of teachers and administrators who have built professional development around research-based strategies and professional learning communities, only to be disappointed by the results. Why? They were focused on the right things. They understood the crucial importance of collegial learning. What they needed was the *how. How do we make our professional learning communities work?*

The solution we developed with these schools is *learning clubs*. If you've been struggling to make the professional learning community concept a reality in your school, or if you're just beginning the process of establishing a professional learning community, learning clubs can help. A learning club is a collaborative support structure that makes the process of establishing and sustaining a professional learning community more manageable for teachers, administrators, and schools. A typical learning club consists of four to eight teachers who meet regularly to talk about and refine their instructional practices.

Learning Clubs and Strategic Teacher PLC Guides: Perfect Together

Over the years, we have found that the members of the most successful learning clubs follow a relatively standard set of guidelines to maximize the power of collaborative learning. In response, we designed the Strategic Teacher PLC Guides around these guidelines. The members of successful learning clubs

- *Concentrate on instructional techniques proven to make a difference.* That's why each Strategic Teacher PLC Guide focuses on a specific strategy backed by both research and classroom practice.

- *Learn new strategies interdependently.* That's why each Strategic Teacher PLC Guide has been designed for use by a team of teachers. Discussion, group reflection, and group processing activities are all built into its structure.

- *Use new strategies in their classrooms.* That's why each Strategic Teacher PLC Guide puts such a high premium on classroom application. Teachers plan lessons, implement them in the classroom, and evaluate the results together.

- *Bring student work back to their learning clubs.* That's why each Strategic Teacher PLC Guide includes one full section dedicated to the analysis of student work.

- *Self-assess throughout the process.* That's why each Strategic Teacher PLC Guide includes strategy implementation milestones that teachers can use to determine where they are and where they need to go next.

But Where Will We Find the Time?

As the research of Bruce Joyce and Beverly Showers (2002) makes clear, learning a new strategy is never as simple as attending a workshop or reading a chapter in a book. If you expect to implement a new strategy successfully in the classroom, then you'll need to commit at least 10–12 hours of embedded professional development time to master that strategy. Here's how some of the schools we work with address the challenge of time:

- Some schools convert their staff meetings, grade-level meetings, or department meetings into learning club sessions.

- Some schools use a portion of their committed professional development days for learning clubs.

- Some schools create intensive summer sessions for their learning clubs.

- Some schools have made a full commitment to the power of job-embedded learning and set aside regular time for learning clubs to meet on a weekly, biweekly, or monthly basis.

Because each school has unique scheduling demands and professional development resources, Strategic Teacher PLC Guides provide maximum flexibility. This guide, for example, is divided into four separate sections:

- Section 1 serves as an introductory tutorial on Reading for Meaning. Between Sections 1 and 2, teachers look for opportunities to incorporate basic elements of the strategy into their instruction.

- Section 2 shows teachers how to plan and implement a Reading for Meaning lesson in their classrooms. Between Sections 2 and 3, teachers implement their lessons in the classroom and work with a critical friend to provide reciprocal feedback on their lessons.

- In Section 3, teachers reflect on how their lessons worked in the classroom. Between Sections 3 and 4, teachers design and implement a new lesson and collect samples of student work.

- Section 4 models a process for analyzing student work and shows teachers how to use this student work to improve instructional decision making.

We recommend that you preview these four sections and develop a schedule that works for all the members of your learning club. *As a final note, make sure you photocopy the lesson planning forms before filling them out (see pp. 58–61). You will need more blank forms as you plan future lessons.*

Good luck and good learning!

Why Reading for Meaning?

This section serves as an introductory tutorial on the Reading for Meaning strategy. In this section, our goals are to help you reflect on your current approach to building students' comprehension skills in your classroom and to explain the Strategic Teacher approach to Reading for Meaning.

In this section you will

- Reflect on your own experiences with reading comprehension strategies.

- Explore the research, principles, and classroom phases that make Reading for Meaning such a powerful strategy for building students' reading and reasoning skills.

- Examine a range of student work and classroom applications that demonstrate the different ways Reading for Meaning can be used to deepen student thinking and build comprehension.

- Experience a model lesson using the Reading for Meaning strategy.

Let's Get Started

Adults tend to forget just how challenging the act of making meaning out of the words on a page can be. Thus, we begin this Strategic Teacher PLC Guide on Reading for Meaning with a few short texts that can put us in better touch with the challenges that many of our students face as readers. We deliberately selected these texts as reminders that understanding what we read is not always a snap. We call the following five texts "An Anthology of Rigorous Readings." Preview all of the readings and then pick two for close reading—the one you believe will be the most challenging, and the one you believe will be the least challenging.

An Anthology of Rigorous Readings

Reading One:

Excerpt from the Federalist Papers, "Concerning the General Power of Taxation," by Alexander Hamilton

It has been already observed that the federal government ought to possess the power of providing for the support of the national forces; in which proposition was intended to be included the expense of raising troops, of building and equipping fleets, and all other expenses in any wise connected with military arrangements and operations. But these are not the only objects to which the jurisdiction of the Union, in respect to revenue, must necessarily be empowered to extend. It must embrace a provision for the support of the national civil list; for the payment of the national debts contracted, or that may be contracted; and, in general, for all those matters which will call for disbursements out of the national treasury. The conclusion is, that there must be interwoven, in the frame of the government, a general power of taxation, in one shape or another.

Reading Two:

"There's a certain Slant of light," by Emily Dickinson

There's a certain Slant of light,
Winter Afternoons —
That oppresses, like the Heft
Of Cathedral Tunes —

Heavenly Hurt, it gives us —
We can find no scar,
But internal difference,
Where the Meanings, are —

None may teach it — Any —
'Tis the Seal Despair —
An imperial affliction
Sent us of the Air —

When it comes, the Landscape listens —
Shadows — hold their breath —
When it goes, 'tis like the Distance
On the look of Death —

Reading Three:

A Description of the Healing Process Adapted from a High School Biology Textbook

Endothelial cells bud and grow from existing blood vessels, undergo canalization, and form a vascular network by connecting to other cell buds. New vessels are all similar in appearance, with thin walls made of endothelium. Protein leaks out of the vessels, bathing the wound area in plasma and providing a rich nutrient medium that promotes rapid cell growth. Once this nutrient medium is established, differentiation can begin. Some vessels will become venules, which are large and have thin walls, while others will become arterioles, which have muscular coats. As granulation tissue steadily changes, some vessels will disappear. Those that remain will become part of the capillary bed.

Reading Four:

Excerpt from *The Souls of Black Folk,* by W. E. B. Du Bois

Between me and the other world there is ever an unasked question: unasked by some through feelings of delicacy; by others through the difficulty of rightly framing it. All, nevertheless, flutter round it. They approach me in a half-hesitant sort of way, eye me curiously or compassionately, and then, instead of saying directly, How does it feel to be a problem? they say, I know an excellent colored man in my town; or, I fought at Mechanicsville; or, Do not these Southern outrages make your blood boil? At these I smile, or am interested, or reduce the boiling to a simmer, as the occasion may require. To the real question, How does it feel to be a problem? I answer seldom a word.

Reading Five:

What Is the Hailstone Sequence? Exploring a Mathematical Mystery

One mystery that has puzzled mathematicians for years is a strange series of numbers known as a hailstone sequence. To create a hailstone sequence, take any positive integer n. If n is even, divide it by 2. If n is odd, multiply it by 3 and add 1. Then, take the result and repeat the process over and over to generate a sequence of numbers. If we apply this procedure to $n = 11$, we get: 34, 17, 52, 26, 13, 40, 20, 10, 5, 16, 8, 4, 2, 1, 4, 2, 1. . . . These sequences are called *hailstone sequences* because the numbers mimic the up-and-down movement of hailstones as they form in clouds.

Notice that the sequence above ends in a repeating pattern—4, 2, 1, 4, 2, 1. . . . It is believed that every value for n will settle into this 4, 2, 1 pattern. But some values generate long sequences before the pattern emerges. For example, $n = 27$ yields 109 numbers before the 4, 2, 1 pattern begins. So what's the mystery? No mathematician has yet proven that *every* positive integer will generate a sequence that eventually settles into a repeating 4, 2, 1 pattern.

So, how did you do? Were your prereading predictions correct? Did the reading you expected to be more challenging end up being more challenging? We'd like you to take a metacognitive approach to your own reading by thinking about this question: *how* did you read your selected texts? What was your mind doing to help you understand what you read? Take a look at the list of reading and thinking skills below. Did you use any of these skills to help you make sense of the more challenging texts? Check off any skills you found yourself using.

Before reading did you . . .

- ☐ Draw forth relevant background knowledge to help you put the reading in context?
- ☐ Make predictions about what the text would say or include?
- ☐ Establish a purpose for reading?

During reading did you . . .

- ☐ Apply criteria that helped you separate critical information from less relevant information?
- ☐ Pay attention to how the ideas were presented and organized?
- ☐ Make notes to help you highlight and clarify important ideas?
- ☐ Form images in your head to help you "see" the content?
- ☐ Note when the text confirmed or refuted your initial ideas or prereading predictions?

After reading did you . . .

- ☐ Reflect on what you read?
- ☐ Try to assess and shore up gaps in your comprehension? (What do I need to better understand?)
- ☐ Look for opportunities to discuss your ideas with other readers?

Now, compare and discuss your list with the members of your learning club. Which skills were used the most? Which were used the least? With your learning club, take a few minutes to discuss and respond to the questions on the following page.

Activity: Thinking About the Skills of Comprehension

1. How did the skills you checked off help you understand the texts you read?

2. What are some ways you teach these skills in your classroom?

3. What are some of the recurring challenges you face in helping students build their reading and reasoning skills?

What Is a Proficient Reader?

So what is a proficient reader? The first answer is—if you checked off several of the skills from the list on page 8—you. Proficient readers use a set of skills to help them derive meaning from even the most difficult texts, a set of skills that has much in common with the list on page 8. What's noteworthy about this list of reading and thinking skills is how it came to be. How do we know that proficient readers use these skills to build their understanding?

The story begins more than 30 years ago, when Dolores Durkin (1978–1979) published an important study with a troubling conclusion about reading instruction. Durkin found that comprehension—the very thing students were being tested for in nearly every classroom—was being taken for granted by teachers. Students were being set up for failure based on a false assumption that the active reading, processing, and thinking that make up comprehension did not need to be taught. As long as students were reading words on a page, it was assumed that they should be "getting it."

Durkin's study helped usher in a new wave in reading research. A new generation of researchers, including Michael Pressley, P. David Pearson, Peter Afflerbach, Ruth Garner, Peter Johnston, John Guthrie, James Baumann, Annemarie Palincsar, Donna Alvermann, and Gerald Duffy began paying close attention to the processes involved in comprehension. A significant number of studies (see, for example, Pressley & Afflerbach, 1995; Wyatt et al., 1993) focused on a question much like the one we asked you: What is your mind doing while you read? By posing this simple but long-overlooked question to skilled readers, these researchers were able to draw some important conclusions about how good readers "read for meaning."

Below are some of the most important findings to emerge from this body of research. As you read through these findings, think about the impact this research might have on your work in reading instruction.

1. Good reading is active reading. Good readers are actively engaged not only while reading but also before reading—when they call up what they already know about the topic and establish a purpose for reading—and after reading, when they reflect on their understanding and seek to deepen it. Michael Pressley (2006) summarizes it this way: "In general, the conscious processing that is excellent reading begins before reading, continues during reading, and persists after reading is completed" (p. 57).

2. Comprehension involves a repertoire of skills, or reading and thinking strategies. Susan Zimmermann and Chryse Hutchins (2003) synthesize the findings of the research on proficient readers by identifying "seven keys to comprehension," a set of skills that includes making connections to background knowledge, drawing inferences, and determining importance.

3. These comprehension skills can be taught successfully to nearly all readers, including young and emerging readers. For example, in *Mosaic of Thought* (2007), Ellin Oliver Keene and Susan Zimmermann show how teachers at all grade levels—including primary-level teachers— teach comprehension skills in their classrooms.

4. A wide body of research shows that teaching students comprehension skills has "a significant and lasting effect on students' understanding" (Keene, 2010, p. 70).

Now that you know a little bit of the story and research behind the list, answer the question in the following activity. Discuss your responses with your learning club.

Activity: Thinking About the Research

> **How might this research affect the way you teach students to "read for meaning"?**

Introducing Reading for Meaning

Reading for Meaning is a strategy built on some of the key findings from the research investigating how proficient readers build deep understanding of the texts they read. But it is more than a reading strategy, and more than a comprehension strategy. When used well, Reading for Meaning helps teachers and students meet the following six crucial learning goals:

GOAL #1:   **Find Main Ideas**
Reading for Meaning helps students locate main ideas when they are explicitly stated, construct main ideas that need to be inferred, and use main ideas to organize important details.

GOAL #2:   **Gather and Evaluate Evidence**
Few strategies put a higher premium on evidence than Reading for Meaning does. Students learn how to put claims to the test by scouring texts (and other sources of information) for evidence that either supports or refutes those claims.

GOAL #3:   **Develop Powerful Explanations and Interpretations**
After students have gathered specific information and evidence, they must turn their findings into clear explanations or compelling interpretations that answer these questions: What's going on here? How do you know? What examples or proof can you offer to support your ideas?

continued

GOAL #4:   **Build Students' Note-Taking Capacities**
Reading for Meaning models a simple but powerful note-taking technique that enables students to distinguish between crucial information and trivial or irrelevant information.

GOAL #5:   **Improve Students' Writing**
With its emphasis on evidence, claims, and positions, Reading for Meaning serves as an ideal strategy for helping students to build their powers as persuasive writers.

GOAL #6:   **Develop Students' Habits of Mind**
In their years of research into the defining characteristics of intelligent behavior and thought, Art Costa and Bena Kallick (2008, 2009) have identified 16 "habits of mind." By nourishing these habits in our students, we give them the tools they need to use their minds well, thus increasing their chance for future success. Using Reading for Meaning in the classroom will help students develop these habits of mind: thinking flexibly; thinking about thinking (metacognition); applying past knowledge to new situations; thinking and communicating with clarity and precision; listening with understanding and empathy; and thinking interdependently.

Answer the question below and then discuss your answer with your learning club.

Activity: The Most Important Goal

Which of the six goals of Reading for Meaning is most important to you, and why?

Reading for Meaning in the Classroom

At the heart of any Reading for Meaning lesson is a set of statements about a text, a group of texts, a word problem, a data chart, a painting, a lab experiment, or just about any other source of information that you want students to think about deeply. Using statements to pique interest and increase students' analytical powers while reading and learning is a technique adapted from Harold Herber's (1978) work with Anticipation Guides. It is important to remember that Reading for Meaning statements need not be true. They can inspire debate ("Teaching is more an art than a science"), encourage speculation ("There are probably more reptiles living in Mexico than in the United States"), or be open to interpretation ("Countee Cullen was deeply hurt by the incident in the poem"). Statements can even be flat-out false. What's important is that students gather evidence that supports or refutes each statement or, as is sometimes the case with particularly rich or open-ended statements, that supports *and* refutes the statement.

Figure 1.1 (pp. 13–17) shows how teachers and students use Reading for Meaning statements in the classroom. The lessons and samples of student work span a wide range of content areas and grade levels. As you examine this Reading for Meaning potpourri, ask yourself, How do these different uses of Reading for Meaning statements deepen student thinking about the content? What effect on student comprehension might they have? How about on classroom discussion? After looking over the potpourri, discuss the sample lessons and student work with a partner. Which applications caught your attention? Which would work best in your classroom? Record your thoughts in the space that follows the potpourri on page 18.

Figure 1.1   Reading for Meaning Potpourri

A primary teacher writes three statements about *Frog and Toad: Dragons and Giants* on an easel to help students learn how to find evidence in a reading.

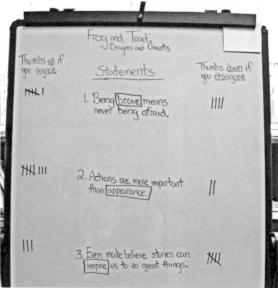

continued

Figure 1.1 (*continued*)

A 2nd grade teacher builds students' word problem–solving skills by asking them to analyze a problem using statements.

Problem: Carly has three sweaters and two pairs of jeans. If she has an orange sweater, a purple sweater, and a red sweater plus a pair of a blue jeans and a pair of black jeans, how many different outfits can she make?

Statements	Agree	Disagree
1. Carly can make an outfit with an orange sweater and a pair of blue jeans.	☐	☐
2. To answer the problem, all you need to do is add.	☐	☐
3. The answer to the problem will be more than three outfits.	☐	☐

A high school English teacher uses Reading for Meaning to help students interpret a scene from *Romeo and Juliet*.

Romeo & Juliet — Act III, Scene II

Agree?	Statements	Your Evidence
yes / no	1. Juliet's soliloquy (lines 1–31) reveals how young and naive she is	
yes / no	2. Juliet's attitude towards Romeo changes over the course of the scene.	
yes / no	3. Juliet cares more about Tybalt's death than Romeo's banishment.	
yes / no	4. Juliet is in control of her emotions.	

Figure 1.1 (*continued*)

A middle school science teacher helps students develop meaningful conclusions during a lab.

GRAVITY LAB STATEMENTS

USE YOUR EXPERIMENTS AND COMPUTER MODELS TO COLLECT EVIDENCE <u>FOR</u> AND <u>AGAINST</u> EACH OF THE FOLLOWING CONCLUSIONS.

1. THE SIZE OF AN OBJECT DOES NOT AFFECT ITS GRAVITATIONAL FORCE.

2. THE CLOSER YOU GET TO AN OBJECT, THE STRONGER THE GRAVITATIONAL FORCE.

3. GRAVITY IS ONLY AN ATTRACTIVE FORCE.

4. IF THE MASS OF ONE OF TWO ATTRACTING OBJECTS IS DOUBLED, THE GRAVITATIONAL FORCE WILL BE DOUBLED.

A 5th grade teacher builds students' data-analysis skills using Reading for Meaning.

Statements	Evidence/Calculations
1. Seattle receives more precipitation in a year than Boston. ☐ Agree ☐ Disagree	
2. Over the course of a year, Denver sees more snow than rain. ☐ Agree ☐ Disagree	
3. On average, January is the coldest month. ☐ Agree ☐ Disagree	
4. If you were spending Independence Day in Boston, the temperature would not be above 81°F. ☐ Agree ☐ Disagree	

City	Avg.	Month											
		JAN	FEB	MAR	APR	MAY	JUN	JUL	AUG	SEP	OCT	NOV	DEC
Boston	*Precip.*	3.6	3.6	3.7	3.6	3.3	3.1	2.8	3.3	3.1	3.3	4.3	4.0
	Low	21	24	31	40	48	58	65	64	56	46	38	26
	High	35	37	45	55	66	76	81	78	72	62	52	40
Denver	*Precip.*	0.5	0.6	1.3	1.7	2.4	1.8	1.9	1.5	1.3	1.0	0.9	0.6
	Low	16	20	25	34	44	52	58	56	47	36	25	17
	High	44	46	52	61	70	81	88	85	76	66	52	44
Seattle	*Precip.*	5.4	4.0	3.5	2.3	1.7	1.5	0.8	1.1	1.9	3.3	5.8	5.9
	Low	35	37	38	41	46	51	55	55	51	45	40	35
	High	45	48	52	57	64	68	75	75	68	58	50	45

Average temperatures recorded in degrees Fahrenheit (°F)
Average precipitation amounts recorded in inches (in.)

A 5th grade teacher builds students' data analysis skills using Reading for Meaning statements. Students analyze the weather data (see inset table) and collect evidence for or against each statement.

continued

Figure 1.1 *(continued)*

An elementary school student analyzes an imaginary creature called a "Woggle" using Reading for Meaning statements.

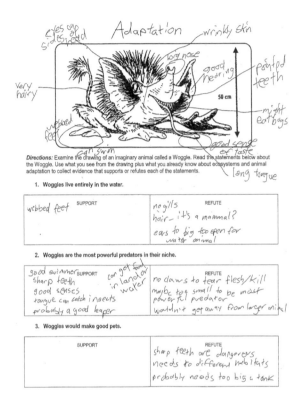

A high school student uses Reading for Meaning as a note-taking technique.

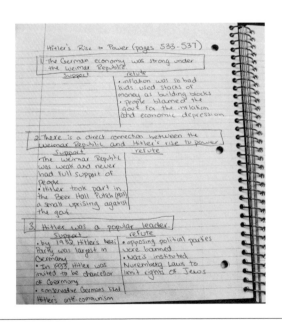

Figure 1.1 (*continued*)

A student in a career and technical education craft skills program creates a Reading for Meaning organizer in her notebook to help her read a text on stonemasonry.

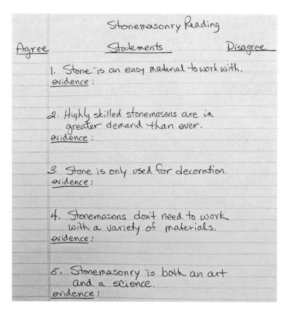

A Spanish teacher uses statements to help students analyze Goya's etching "And There's Nothing to Be Done."

Mira la aguafuerte. Lea las declaraciones abajo y a recolectar evidencia "a favor" o "en contra" de cada declaracion.

Look at the etching. Read the statements below and collect evidence "for" or "against" each statement.

Evidencia a Favor	Declaraciones	Evidencia en Contra
	1. La artista no es optimista de la guerra.	
	1. The artist is not optimistic about the war.	
	2. Los soldados estan haciendo su sustantivo.	
	2. The soldiers are doing their duty.	
	3. El prisionero es desafiante.	
	3. The prisoner is defiant.	

Activity: Looking at the Potpourri

1. How do statements deepen student thinking?

2. What effects would they likely have on comprehension and on classroom discussion?

3. Which applications caught your attention?

4. Which applications would work best in your classroom?

We all want our students to read for meaning—to be able to understand new ideas, make inferences, and support their thinking with evidence. To help us achieve this goal, let's turn our attention to the four principles of Reading for Meaning. Each principle is tied to a finding from the research on proficient readers. You'll notice that the four *principles* of Reading for Meaning are closely aligned with the four classroom *phases* of Reading for Meaning. Leading your students through these four phases is essential for ensuring students' effective use of the strategy in the classroom. A classroom poster highlighting the role that students play during a Reading for Meaning lesson is included with this guide. Figure 1.2 shows the four principles and corresponding four phases of Reading for Meaning.

Figure 1.2   The Four Principles and Phases of Reading for Meaning

Principle One: Before You Get Reading, Get Ready

Good readers don't just plunge blindly into a reading. Instead, they take time to prepare for reading, calling up relevant background knowledge, making predictions, and establishing their purpose for reading.

Phase One: Introduction of the Text and Topic

Help prepare students for active reading by

- Establishing the purpose for reading (e.g., "Today we'll be reading a selection called 'Cold-Blooded Blues' to help us learn more about the challenges that reptiles face in maintaining their body temperature").

- Helping students tap into past knowledge that they can apply to the reading to come.

- Providing additional background information if necessary to help students contextualize the reading.

- Introducing the Reading for Meaning statements.

  - If statements are general in nature (e.g., "Relocation is an inhumane policy"), have students decide whether they agree or disagree with each statement.

  - If statements are text-specific and will lead to blind guessing (e.g., "The author wants us to feel sorry for the mouse"), have students use the statements to make predictions about the text.

- Using the poster included with this guide to help students understand what to do during each phase of the strategy.

continued

Figure 1.2 (*continued*)

Principle Two: Read Like You Mean It

Quality reading implies ongoing, active engagement of the mind rather than passive reception of information. That's why proficient readers work to separate relevant information from irrelevant information, make notes, and check their comprehension while reading.

Phase Two: Active Reading

Encourage students to read the text actively and with purpose by

- Modeling the evidence-gathering process using a sample statement.

- Reminding students to look for textual information that relates specifically to the statements.

- Having students record information that either supports or refutes the statements on a Reading for Meaning organizer (see below):

Evidence For	Statements	Evidence Against
	Hurricanes occur only in the Atlantic Ocean.	
	Hurricanes behave differently over water than they do over land.	
	Scientists agree on why hurricanes are occurring more frequently than they did 50 years ago.	
	A hurricane could never reach as far north as Maine.	

Figure 1.2 (*continued*)

Principle Three: Just Because You're Done Reading Doesn't Mean You're Done Reading

Turning reading into learning means giving students the opportunity to look back on the text, revisit predictions, discuss evidence, and reflect on how the text has influenced their understanding. This post-reading phase is also an ideal time to review the reading strategies students used and to encourage students to talk about how they can use these strategies on their own.

Principle Four: Put Reading to Use

The most powerful form of reading is applied reading—reading that leads to a product in which students synthesize what they have learned.

Phase Three: Reflection and Discussion

- Build students' capacity for interdependent thinking by having them meet in small groups to discuss the statements, their responses, and what they learned from the reading.

- Circulate around the room and help groups by encouraging them to try to reach consensus on whether the text supports or refutes each statement.

- Survey students' positions and lead a whole-class discussion on the textual evidence and its relationship to each statement.

- Build in time for metacognitive reflection by leading a review and discussion of the Reading for Meaning process: What reading and thinking skills did you use? How did they help? How might you use these skills independently?

Phase Four: Synthesis

Ask students to apply what they have learned to a writing task or project.

The Strategy in Action

Now let's experience a complete Reading for Meaning lesson designed by a teacher. Angel Sapporo, a high school English teacher, is conducting a thematic literature lesson. The title of the unit, which Angel has borrowed from a famous line in *Macbeth*, is "Cabin'd, Cribb'd, Confin'd: How Authors Help Us Understand What It Means to Be Trapped." Using Hamlin Garland's "Under the Lion's Paw," Charlotte Perkins Gilman's "The Yellow Wallpaper," and poems by Langston Hughes, Angel and his students have been investigating the different ways people can feel trapped—by racial and gender roles, by cultural expectations, and by social and economic barriers. Today, Angel and his students are reading a short story by the Russian author Anton Chekhov to see what new insights they can gather about how and why authors create this feeling of being trapped.

Angel is using Reading for Meaning to help students

- Review what they already know about the theme of being trapped and apply that knowledge to Chekhov's story.

- Develop and discuss their insights into the story.

- Take a position on the story and defend that position using textual evidence.

The Model Lesson

Note to participants: As you review this lesson, keep in mind the principles of Reading for Meaning, the role of the students, the role of the teacher, and the goals of the strategy. We also encourage you to *be* the student by completing the student activities throughout the lesson. You'll notice that we have included "You Try It" activities throughout, as well as space for you to record "Your Thoughts on the Model Lesson" at the end (p. 31). This is part of the process we call "Do, Look, Learn," which puts the power of metacognition, or thinking about thinking, to work. Too often, we go through the motions of learning a new strategy or technique without reflecting on our own thought process. So as you "do" the lesson, "look" in on your own thought process and see what you can "learn" from your own experiences.

Phase One: Introduction of the Text and Topic

Angel begins the lesson by saying, "OK, so we've been busy looking into how authors create the feeling of being trapped. And as we were exploring this theme, some of us started asking why so many authors seem to be drawn to this theme. After all, stories about being trapped certainly aren't feel-good stories. They don't lend themselves to happy, Hollywood-style endings. So what are some of the reasons authors spend their time and talent on this theme of being trapped? Let's review."

Using the poems and stories from the unit to guide them, Angel and his students review their discussion on why authors write about being trapped. Angel records the reasons they've come up with on the board:

Why do authors write about being trapped?

- To show injustice and bring about social change.

- To express their frustration.

- To help readers identify with others.

- To create a conversation about difficult issues like race, gender, and inequality.

Next, Angel says, "Today we're going to read the final story in this unit. This story is by the great Russian author Anton Chekhov. You'll notice that the story is very short. One thing to keep your eye on is how Chekhov is able to create such a great effect with so few words. Of course, we're also going to be paying close attention to how and why Chekhov creates the feeling of being trapped in his story." Angel then distributes copies of a Reading for Meaning organizer to his students (see Figure 1.3, p. 24) and reveals that the story they'll be reading is called "A Nincompoop."

Figure 1.3   Reading for Meaning Organizer

Evidence For	Statements	Evidence Against
	Julia accepts her wages from the narrator without protest.	
	Julia is used to being powerless.	
	Julia respects the narrator.	
	The narrator is more interested in conducting a social experiment than in teaching Julia a life lesson.	
	Chekhov would disapprove of Hemingway's "iceberg" theory of literature (most of what's happening lies below the surface).	

Angel asks the students to preview the five statements about "A Nincompoop" on the organizer and to use the statements to make two or three predictions about the story.

You Try It: Making Predictions

Use the space below to make two or three predictions about "A Nincompoop" based on the statements in Figure 1.3.

1.

2.

3.

Phase Two: Active Reading

Angel's students have used the Reading for Meaning strategy several times before, so they are familiar with their roles. Angel encourages students to refer to the Reading for Meaning poster (included with this guide) to help keep themselves focused.

Students read "A Nincompoop" on their own. As they read the story, they collect evidence on their Reading for Meaning organizers (see Figure 1.3). Angel reminds students that whenever they discover something in the story that relates to one of the statements, they should stop; ask themselves, "Does this information support the statement or refute the statement?"; and record the information in the appropriate column.

You Try It: Collecting Evidence

As you read "A Nincompoop," record evidence from the story that either supports or refutes each statement in the Reading for Meaning organizer (Figure 1.3).

A Nincompoop
by Anton Chekhov

A few days ago I asked my children's governess, Julia Vassilyevna, to come into my study.

"Sit down, Julia Vassilyevna," I said. "Let's settle our accounts. Although you most likely need some money, you stand on ceremony and won't ask for it yourself. Now then, we agreed on thirty rubles a month. . . . "

"Forty."

"No, thirty. I made a note of it. I always pay the governess thirty. Now then, you've been here two months, so. . . . "

"Two months and five days."

"Exactly two months. I made a specific note of it. That means you have sixty rubles coming to you. Subtract nine Sundays . . . you know you didn't work with Koyla on Sundays, you only took walks. And three holidays. . . . "

Julia Vassilyevna flushed a deep red and picked at the flounce of her dress, but—not a word.

"Three holidays, therefore take off twelve rubles. Four days Kolya was sick and there were no lessons, as you were occupied only with Vanya. Three days you had a toothache and my wife gave you permission not to work after lunch. Twelve and seven—nineteen. Subtract . . . that leaves . . . hmm . . . forty-one rubles. Correct?"

Julia Vassilyevna's left eye reddened and filled with moisture. Her chin trembled; she coughed nervously and blew her nose, but—not a word.

"Around New Year's you broke a teacup and saucer; take off two rubles. The cup cost more, it was an heirloom, but—let it go. When didn't I take a loss! Then due to your neglect, Kolya climbed a tree and tore his jacket; take away ten. Also due to your heedlessness the maid stole Vanya's shoes. You ought to watch everything. You get paid for it. So, that means five more rubles off. The tenth of January I gave you ten rubles. . . . "

"You didn't," whispered Julia Vassilyevna.

"But I made a note of it."

"Well . . . all right."

"Take twenty-seven from forty-one—that leaves fourteen."

Both eyes filled with tears. Perspiration appeared on the thin, pretty little nose. Poor girl!

"Only once was I given any money," she said in a trembling voice, "and that was by your wife. Three rubles, nothing more."

"Really? You see now, and I didn't make a note of it. Take three from fourteen . . . leaves eleven. Here's your money, my dear. Three, three, three, one and one. Here it is!"

I handed her eleven rubles. She took them and with trembling fingers stuffed them into her pocket.

"*Merci*," she whispered.

I jumped and started pacing the room. I was overcome with anger.

"For what, this—'*merci*'?" I asked.

"For the money."

"But you know I've cheated you, for God's sake—robbed you! I have actually stolen from you! *Why* this '*merci*'?"

"In my other places they didn't give me anything at all."

"They didn't give you anything? No wonder! I played a little joke on you, a cruel lesson just to teach you. . . . I'm going to give you the entire eighty rubles! Here they are in an envelope all ready for you. . . . Is it really possible to be so spineless? Why don't you protest? Why be silent? Is it possible in this world to be without teeth and claws—to be such a nincompoop?"

She smiled crookedly and I read her expression: "It is possible."

I asked her pardon for the cruel lesson and, to her great surprise, gave her the eighty rubles. She murmured her little "*merci*" several times and went out. I looked after her and thought: "How easy it is to crush the weak in this world!"

Figure 1.4 shows the evidence one student collected from "A Nincompoop." How does the student's evidence compare with yours?

Figure 1.4 Student's Completed Reading for Meaning Organizer

Evidence For	Statements	Evidence Against
• "Not a word" • She takes only 11 rubles when she's owed 80. • She says "Merci."	Julia accepts her wages from the narrator without protest.	In the beginning, she protests • Forty rubles a month. • She counters him: – "Two months and five days." – "You didn't."
• "In my other places they didn't give me anything at all." • She isn't able to stand up for herself even though she's being taken advantage of.	Julia is used to being powerless.	
• She says "Merci." • She stops protesting and accepts what he gives her.	Julia respects the narrator.	
• "How easy it is to crush the weak in this world!" • Lesson seems more for his own curiosity than for her. • He's cruel to her.	The narrator is more interested in conducting a social experiment than in teaching Julia a life lesson.	• But . . . he does give her the money and tells her he's teaching her a lesson.
	Chekhov would disapprove of Hemingway's "iceberg" theory of literature (most of what's happening lies below the surface).	• He would almost definitely approve of the "iceberg theory." All that's going on inside Julia's head is not revealed to the reader.

Phase Three: Reflection and Discussion

Once students have read the story and made their notes on their organizers, they meet in small discussion groups. Students review each statement and explain their position on the statement using evidence from the story. Some of the discussion groups get rather lively, so Angel reminds students that disagreement is natural, but that all positions should be treated with respect and should be based on evidence from the text.

You Try It: Reflecting and Discussing

> With your learning club, review each statement from the Reading for Meaning organizer (Figure 1.3) and discuss the evidence you collected in support or refutation of each statement. Are there any significant disagreements? What might be the cause of these disagreements? What can everyone agree on?

After a few minutes of small-group discussion, Angel reconvenes the class for a whole-class discussion. During the discussion, Angel asks students to share their ideas about the story, about how Chekhov handles the theme of being trapped, and about their own thinking and reading processes.

Phase Four: Synthesis

"OK," says Angel. "Now it's time to develop your own interpretation of this wonderful little story. Take a second look at our four reasons authors write about being trapped [see p. 23]. Which of these reasons do you believe was foremost on Chekhov's mind when he wrote 'A Nincompoop'? Or do you think Chekhov had something else in mind?"

After reviewing the four reasons carefully, students begin their task of writing a brief essay with three guidelines in mind:

1. State your position clearly and up front.

2. Include at least three specific pieces of evidence from the story in your essay.

3. Include at least one possible counterargument to your position and defend your position against it.

You Try It: Synthesizing Your Learning

With your learning club, discuss your position. Do you believe Chekhov was most interested in revealing injustice to promote social change, expressing frustration, helping the reader identify with Julia, or creating a conversation about a difficult issue? Use the space below to collect your ideas from the discussion.

Your Thoughts on the Model Lesson

THOUGHTWORK

Before the Next Section

Take a moment to reflect on what you have learned so far by answering the questions below.

Activity: Reflecting on Section 1

1. How did Reading for Meaning help Angel achieve his lesson goals?

2. How do the phases of the strategy support the principles behind the strategy?

3. How is Reading for Meaning similar to what you already do with your students?

In the next section, you will be planning your own Reading for Meaning lesson. To prepare, you should do the following things before you move on:

- Keep an eye out for students who make claims and use evidence in your classroom. What do you notice them doing? How comfortable are they with the process?

- As you teach over the coming weeks, keep track of those times when you might use Reading for Meaning statements. Make note of those instances.

- Compile all the materials you'll need to plan a Reading for Meaning lesson (e.g., content, readings, standards to cover) and bring them to the next learning club meeting.

Planning a Lesson

The goal in this section is to work with a partner to develop a Reading for Meaning lesson for your students.

In this section you will

■ Examine and learn from sample lessons and planning forms designed by other teachers.

■ Learn how you can design Reading for Meaning statements to build specific reading and reasoning skills. If you are a math teacher using Reading for Meaning with word problems, you will learn how you can design statements that build students' reasoning and problem-solving skills.

■ Plan a complete Reading for Meaning lesson for your classroom.

■ Learn classroom tips to ensure highly effective implementation of Reading for Meaning in your classroom.

Samples of Reading for Meaning Lessons

This jigsaw-based task is designed to increase each learning club member's sense of responsibility for learning by making each an "expert" in one part of the content. The experts then meet to share their acquired knowledge.

On the following pages, you will find a matrix organizer (Figure 2.1) followed by four sample Reading for Meaning lessons: a 1st grade language arts/nutrition lesson, a 3rd grade mathematics lesson, a middle school history lesson, and a high school physics lesson. Here's how you and your learning club will use these resources to complete this activity:

1. Form a partnership with two other members of your learning club.

2. Read "Sample Lesson 1: 1st Grade Language Arts/Nutrition." Together, review the completed column for this lesson in Figure 2.1. You and your partners will be completing the remaining columns in Figure 2.1.

3. Assign each of the remaining lessons to a different member of the group.

4. Read your assigned lesson carefully. As you read it, underline key ideas, phrases, and interesting points. Use the margins, a blank sheet of paper, or the space below to make a set of notes that will help you teach what you have read back to your partners.

5. Rejoin your partners. Each of you will teach the content of your assigned sample lesson to the other partners. Finally, you will work together to complete Figure 2.1.

Activity: Notes on Your Assigned Lesson

Figure 2.1   Activity: Identifying the Classroom Phases

Classroom Phase	Sample Lesson 1	Sample Lesson 2	Sample Lesson 3	Sample Lesson 4
Introduction of the Text and Topic How did the teacher establish the purpose for reading and activate background knowledge?	Colin engages students in a discussion about their own eating habits.			
Active Reading How did the teacher help students turn reading into an active search?	He has them put on their "detective hats." He reads aloud four statements on an easel and stops at key points to help students find evidence for or against the statements.			
Reflection and Discussion How did the teacher help students look back on the reading and discuss and refine their ideas?	He discusses with students how it felt to read like a detective and what they learned from the reading about healthy eating.			
Synthesis How did students apply their learning?	Students create a balanced meal they would enjoy, including one new food that they would like to try.			

Sample Lesson 1: 1st Grade Language Arts/Nutrition

Gregory the Terrible Eater

Colin Goldberg's 1st graders are learning about healthy eating habits. Today, Colin is reading aloud Mitchell Sharmat's *Gregory the Terrible Eater* to his students. Before starting to read, Colin poses questions about eating habits to the class: What did you eat for breakfast? Who chooses what you eat? What is the difference between good and bad eating habits? After a few minutes of discussion, Colin tells students that they will be reading a book about eating habits called *Gregory the Terrible Eater*. Next to Colin is an easel on which four statements are written (see Figure 2.2).

Figure 2.2   Reading for Meaning Statements on an Easel

Proof For	Statements	Proof Against
	Gregory is a healthy eater.	
	Gregory eats what humans should eat.	
	Gregory is eating the right foods for a goat.	
	Gregory's parents are happy once he eats the foods they like.	

After reading the statements to the class, Colin tells students to put on their "detective hats" and look for clues in the story that can help them decide whether each statement is true or false. At key points during the reading, Colin stops and asks students if they notice any clues that tell them whether a statement is true or false. Colin records students' observations on the easel. If the information suggests that a statement is true, he writes it in the "Proof For" column. If the information suggests that a statement is false, he writes it in the "Proof Against" column.

After completing the story and entering students' proof on the easel, Colin and the class discuss their findings. They talk about how good reading is like being a detective and discuss what it means to eat balanced meals.

To conclude the lesson, Colin says, "Although people shouldn't eat tin cans and cardboard boxes like the goats in *Gregory the Terrible Eater*, it is a good idea to try new foods like Gregory." For homework, Colin asks students to cut out or draw pictures of foods to create a balanced meal that they would enjoy. Students' meals must include something new that they would be willing to try.

Sample Lesson 2: 3rd Grade Mathematics
Solving Word Problems

Third grade teacher Heather Alvarez uses Reading for Meaning statements to help her students analyze and develop a plan of attack for mathematical word problems. Because she does this regularly with her students, they are familiar with using statements to improve their problem-solving skills.

Before introducing today's problem, Heather asks students to share experiences they have had with haircuts: How often do you get your hair cut? What kind of haircut would you never get? Is there one type of cut you like best? Did you ever get a really bad haircut and couldn't wait for your hair to grow back? By having students share ideas and humorous stories about haircuts, Heather increases students' engagement in the lesson.

Next, Heather explains that today's word problem will focus on haircuts and the rate at which hair grows. Because a key learning goal of Heather's is to help students distinguish between relevant and irrelevant information in word problems, she works with students to define the terms *relevant information* and *irrelevant information*. Then, she introduces the word problem: *Most 3rd graders get their hair cut four times a year. Human hair grows at a rate of about 0.5 inches a month. If you get 2 inches of hair cut off during a year, about how much longer will your hair be at the end of that year?*

In addition to teaching the key learning goal (distinguishing between relevant and irrelevant information while solving a word problem), Heather wants to foster collaborative problem solving. That's why she has students gather in their learning groups and use the statements in Figure 2.3 to help them figure out what information they need to focus on to solve the problem.

Figure 2.3 Reading for Meaning Organizer for a Word Problem

	Agree	Disagree
1. The first sentence contains relevant information.		
2. Human hair grows at a rate of 1 inch every 2 months.		
3. To solve this problem, you need to find out how much hair grows in a year.		
4. You need to do only one operation to solve this problem.		

In their groups, students analyze the problem and the statements, decide whether they agree or disagree with each statement, and discuss their thinking with one another. Together, students work to resolve their differences over each statement. If they cannot come to a consensus on a statement, Heather asks them to rewrite the statement so that they all agree on it. The group members then work together to solve the actual word problem.

After all the learning groups have completed the word problem, the class reconvenes to share discoveries and solutions. Heather makes sure that during the discussion, students use the vocabulary words *relevant* and *irrelevant* as they explain their thinking.

Finally, Heather helps students synthesize their learning by asking each student to create and solve a hair-growth problem that includes both relevant and irrelevant information. Students exchange their problems with a partner and identify the relevant and irrelevant information in their partner's problem. Partners then solve each other's problems and share their solutions.

Sample Lesson 3: Middle School History

The Gettysburg Address

As part of his U.S. history course, 8th grade teacher Robert Bukowski has students conduct close readings of texts that changed American history. Today, Robert and his students are studying perhaps the most famous presidential address ever delivered: the Gettysburg Address. Robert begins by distributing to each student a Reading for Meaning organizer, which includes five statements about the Gettysburg Address, and asks students to preview these statements and tap into their prior knowledge about Abraham Lincoln, the Civil War, and the Gettysburg Address to make some predictions about what they will find in the text.

Once students have made their predictions, they begin reading. As they read, they collect evidence on their organizers that either supports or refutes each statement. Figure 2.4 shows a partially filled-in organizer containing evidence that one student collected as proof against the first statement, *Lincoln believes that the soldiers have died in vain.*

After reading, students meet in readers' groups to discuss the reading, the statements, and the evidence they collected, working to reach agreement on the accuracy of each statement. During this time, Robert circulates around the room to listen to group members negotiate their ideas. When disagreement occurs, Robert coaches the group in using evidence to justify opinions. After the small-group discussion, the class convenes to share insights about the content and reactions to the process. For homework, Robert asks students to develop a retelling of the Gettysburg Address that a 3rd grader could understand.

As Robert and his students continue to read *Texts That Changed American History* throughout the year, he teaches students how they can use Reading for Meaning independently, as a way to work through difficult readings: whenever a text becomes confusing, students can stop reading and create a short statement about the passage's overall meaning. Students can then use their statement to help them figure out whether the reading supports or refutes their belief.

Figure 2.4   Reading for Meaning Organizer for the Gettysburg Address

Proof For	Statements	Proof Against
	1. Lincoln believes that the soldiers have died in vain. Agree ☐ Disagree ☑	• "gave their lives that this nation might live" • "The brave men, living and dead, who struggled here, have consecrated it. . . ." • "we here highly resolve that these dead shall not have died in vain. . . ."
	2. Lincoln is convinced that great nations survive challenges. Agree ☐ Disagree ☐	
	3. Lincoln sees a clear relationship between the past and the present. Agree ☐ Disagree ☐	
	4. A good slogan for the Gettysburg Address would be "We can work it out." Agree ☐ Disagree ☐	
	5. Lincoln's intent is to make Americans feel guilty about the war. Agree ☐ Disagree ☐	

Sample Lesson 4: High School Physics

Galileo and Pendulums

Brooke Strasser uses Reading for Meaning in her physics classes to help her students understand challenging concepts and texts. Today she is using the strategy for a lesson on the mathematical principles and scientific forces involved in the swing of a pendulum. Brooke begins her lesson with a mini-demonstration: she sets two different pendulums in motion, one with a long string and one with a short string. She asks students to observe each pendulum and record any differences they note in the behavior of each.

Next, Brooke distributes a Reading for Meaning organizer with five statements (see Figure 2.5). She asks students to use both their background knowledge and their observations from the mini-demonstration to decide whether they agree or disagree with each statement.

Figure 2.5   Reading for Meaning Organizer for Physics

Agree	Mathematics is a tool that scientists use to explain things.		Disagree
	Support	Refute	
	Observing is more than looking.		
	Support	Refute	
	The weight of a pendulum has a direct effect on the periods of the pendulum's swing.		
	Support	Refute	
	The time it takes for one swing of a pendulum is a result of the pendulum's length: the longer the length, the faster the swing.		
	Support	Refute	

Figure 2.5 (*continued*)

Agree	For every second it takes a pendulum to swing back and forth, the length of the pendulum is equal to a number the square of the time.		Disagree
	Support	Refute	

Students then gather into small groups to read about Galileo and the observations and discoveries he made while working with pendulums. Students collect evidence to either support or refute each statement. Brooke also allows students to go to her desk and experiment with the two pendulums she used for her mini-demonstration. As she walks around the room, Brooke overhears students discussing their amazement over the fact that the weight of a pendulum has no direct effect on the periods of its swing. Another group comments on how experimenting with the pendulums made the reading much easier to understand.

Brooke gathers her students so that they can recap their findings, reflect on their initial hypotheses, and note how their ideas have changed or been confirmed as a result of reading and experimenting. For homework, Brooke asks students to examine the three different graphs shown in Figure 2.6. Students must choose the graph that best depicts what Galileo discovered about the behavior of pendulums and include a justification for their choice.

Figure 2.6   Which Graph Depicts Galileo's Discovery About Pendulums?

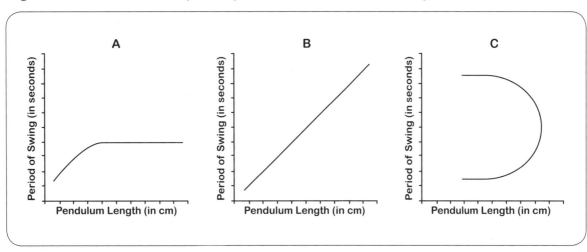

How did you do filling in the Reading for Meaning organizer from Figure 2.1? Check your work against the completed organizer in Figure 2.7.

Figure 2.7   Completed Organizer

Classroom Phase	Sample Lesson 1	Sample Lesson 2	Sample Lesson 3	Sample Lesson 4
Introduction of the Text and Topic How did the teacher establish the purpose for reading and activate background knowledge?	Colin engages students in a discussion about their own eating habits.	Heather asks students to share their "haircut" experiences. She connects their experiences to today's word problem, with a focus on relevant and irrelevant information.	Robert has students preview five statements and use their prior knowledge to make predictions about the Gettysburg Address.	Brooke demonstrates the swings of two pendulums with different lengths and asks students to hypothesize about factors that affect the swing. Students decide whether they agree or disagree with the five statements they're given.
Active Reading How did the teacher help students turn reading into an active search?	He has them put on their "detective hats." He reads aloud four statements on an easel and stops at key points to help students find evidence for or against the statements.	She has students work in groups, using the statements to figure out what information they need to solve the problem. Students try to reach a consensus on each statement and then work together to solve the problem.	He has students collect evidence on their organizers that either supports or refutes each statement.	She breaks students into small groups and the students use the text and experiment with the pendulums to collect evidence related to each statement.

Figure 2.7   (*continued*)

Classroom Phase	Sample Lesson 1	Sample Lesson 2	Sample Lesson 3	Sample Lesson 4
Reflection and Discussion How did the teacher help students look back on the reading and discuss and refine their ideas?	He discusses with students how it felt to read like a detective and what they learned from the reading about healthy eating.	Students discuss their thinking and insights. Heather helps students use the key vocabulary terms *relevant* and *irrelevant* in their explanations.	Students meet in readers' groups to discuss the reading, statements, and evidence. Robert circulates and coaches struggling groups. Robert leads a whole-class discussion about the content and process.	The teacher asks students to recap their findings and note how their initial ideas have changed or been confirmed.
Synthesis How did students apply their learning?	Students create a balanced meal they would enjoy, including one new food that they would like to try.	Students create their own word problem, which must include irrelevant information.	Students develop a retelling of the Gettysburg Address for a 3rd grader. Robert teaches students how to use Reading for Meaning on their own as a way to manage difficult readings.	Students examine three graphs and choose the one that depicts Galileo's discoveries about pendulums. Students must back their choice with evidence.

Customizing Reading for Meaning Statements to Meet Specific Objectives

Reading for Meaning statements are extraordinarily flexible tools for building students' reading and critical thinking skills. Figure 2.8 shows how teachers of a wide variety of content areas and grade levels use statements to help students build 12 different reading skills and overcome common reading challenges. As you examine the figure, think about how you might use different types of statements to enhance your Reading for Meaning lessons. When you have completed your review of Figure 2.8, answer the questions that follow it. Discuss your insights and responses with your learning club.

Figure 2.8   Building Focus Skills with 12 Types of Reading for Meaning Statements

Focus Skill	How to Build It	Sample Statements
Forming Main Ideas	Develop statements that require students to think about the overall meaning.	• The author's main point is that film noir is a style, not a technique. • A good title for this piece would be "We Can Work It Out."
Vocabulary Comprehension	Develop statements that help students use context clues to determine a word's meaning.	• The villagers were surprised that the elephant was so large. [This statement is designed to help students figure out what *marveled* means in the sentence "All the villagers marveled at the size of the elephant."] • Portuguese sailors used the *astrolabe* to help them calculate where they were on the Earth's surface.
Inference	Develop statements that compel students to "read between the lines."	• There are probably more reptiles living in Kansas than there are in Canada. • We can tell that Pooh and Piglet have been friends for a long time.
Visualization/ Forming Mental Images	Develop statements that draw students' attention to image-laden portions of the text.	• A good physical representation of a geometric point would be the tip of a pin. • The author's language helps me imagine what the inside of an aerospace laboratory looks like.
Making a Case	Develop statements that ask students to take a strong position.	• Relocation is an inhumane policy. • Insects are more helpful than harmful.

Figure 2.8 (*continued*)

Focus Skill	How to Build It	Sample Statements
Appreciating Style, Technique, and Genre	Develop statements that focus attention on how the text is written or how well it represents a particular genre.	• The author of the editorial fails to anticipate possible counterarguments. • Lincoln's language conceals the horrors of the battlefield at Gettysburg. • The story of John Henry is an example of a tall tale.
Making Interdisciplinary Connections	Develop statements that include concepts from other disciplines.	• Francis Bacon would approve of Batman's notion of private justice. • Figuring out what's wrong with a car requires using all the steps in the scientific method.
Exploring Metaphors, Similes, and Symbols	Develop statements that help students see how ideas can be represented meta-phorically.	• A colony is a lot like a child. • A good symbol for the Mastery style of learning would be a paper clip.
Empathizing	Develop statements that encourage students to identify with others' feelings and situations.	• Countee Cullen was deeply hurt by the incident in the poem. • The author wants us to feel sorry for the mouse. • The National Baseball Hall of Fame has treated "Shoeless" Joe Jackson unfairly.
Connecting the Reading to a New Context	Develop statements that require students to explore themes and ideas in a new context.	• The Little Prince will make a good king one day. • The Second Amendment is outdated.
Understanding a Process or Procedure	Develop statements that ask students to apply or analyze a sequence or procedure.	• Based on this scenario, we can conclude that the officers did not follow the proper procedure for collecting and documenting evidence. • The best way to solve this word problem is to use the "guess-and-check" method.
Developing a Personal Perspective	Develop statements that invite students' values and beliefs into the conversation.	• Emerson's feelings about personal responsibility are much like my own. • My life would be very different if Thomas Edison hadn't been an inventor.

Source: From *The Strategic Teacher: Selecting the Right Research-Based Strategy for Every Lesson* (pp. 87–89), by H. F. Silver, R. W. Strong, and M. J. Perini, 2007, Alexandria, VA: ASCD. © 2007 by Thoughtful Education Press. Adapted with permission.

Do you have any new insights about Reading for Meaning and Reading for Meaning statements? Answer the questions below and then discuss your responses with your learning club.

Activity: New Insights

1. What new insights about Reading for Meaning statements do you have?

2. Which types of statements are you most eager to include in your lessons? Why?

3. Can you write a statement or two for a lesson you teach that builds one or more of these focus skills? Try it out.

Teacher Talk: Planning a Word Problem–Based Reading for Meaning Lesson

Reading for Meaning can be used to great effect in the mathematics classroom, especially as a way to increase students' reasoning and problem-solving skills when working with word problems. To see how, let's take the following word problem as a model:

> A train containing cars and trucks is en route to an auto dealership in Bowling Green. Before the train arrives, the owner of a group of dealerships receives an invoice showing that a total of 160 vehicles will be delivered to her four locations. Unfortunately, the portion of the invoice detailing how many of each kind of vehicle there are is missing. Because she knows you know algebra, the owner asks for your help. The invoice states that the total mass of vehicles is 182,800 kilograms. Each truck weighs 1,400 kg, while each car weighs 1,000 kg. How many cars and how many trucks will be delivered?

Now let's look at how the teacher designed five Reading for Meaning statements to focus her students' attention on

- *The Facts of the Problem*
    Statement 1: Trucks have a greater mass than cars.

    Statement 2: We already know the total number of vehicles to be delivered.

- *The Process for Solving the Problem*
    Statement 3: The best way to solve this problem is to set up an equation with a single variable.

- *The Hidden Questions Embedded in the Problem*
    Statement 4: The fact that there are four dealerships is irrelevant to finding a solution.

- *The Answer to the Problem*
    Statement 5: The solution will require two different answers.

Source: From *The Strategic Teacher: Selecting the Right Research-Based Strategy for Every Lesson* (p. 91), by H. F. Silver, R. W. Strong, and M. J. Perini, 2007, Alexandria, VA: ASCD. © 2007 by Thoughtful Education Press. Lesson description adapted with permission.

Sample Planning Forms

Now it is time to plan your own Reading for Meaning lesson. To help you plan your lesson, we have included two sets of completed planning forms as references. Sample Planning Form 1 (Figure 2.9) was completed by Robert Bukowski, the middle school history teacher who developed the lesson on the Gettysburg Address. Sample Planning Form 2 (Figure 2.10) represents the work of Heather Alvarez, the 3rd grade teacher who designed the Reading for Meaning lesson around the haircut problem.

Teacher Talk: A Word About Purpose

When you look at the teachers' planning forms for the sample lessons, you'll notice that each used a special framework for defining the purpose of his or her lesson that looks like this:

Knowledge	Habits of Mind*
What key information and facts do students need to know?	What habits of mind do you want to foster?
Understanding	**Skills**
What big ideas, generalizations, or principles do students need to understand?	What skills do students need to develop?

We call this framework a *learning window* (Silver & Perini, 2010), and we have found that using it to clarify purpose leads to richer, more integrated, and better-designed lessons.

*For a complete list of the 16 habits of mind, see the Appendix (p. 87).

Figure 2.9   Sample Planning Form 1: Middle School History

Step 1: Choose the Text

Select a text, a group of texts, or other information you want students to understand deeply. (Remember: Reading for Meaning lessons can be designed around paintings, lectures, data charts, lab experiments, demonstrations, and many other sources of information.) We'll be focusing on the Gettysburg Address as part of our investigation into "Texts That Changed American History."	**Why? How does the text relate to your standards or instructional objectives?** Teaching students how to read primary documents supports these Common Core State Standards: [RH.6-8.1] Cite specific textual evidence to support analysis of primary and secondary sources. [RH.6-8.2] Determine the main ideas or information of a primary or secondary source; provide an accurate summary of the source distinct from prior knowledge or opinions.

Step 2: Clarify the Purpose of the Lesson

Knowledge	**Habits of Mind**
Students will know • The key points of the Gettysburg Address (for a retelling).	Students will develop the habits of • Applying past knowledge to new situations. • Thinking and communicating with clarity and precision.
Understanding	**Skills**
Students will understand • The deep relationship between the Gettysburg Address and the fundamental ideals of the U.S. government. • Why the Gettysburg Address is one of the most important presidential addresses ever delivered.	Students will be able to • Find and use supporting evidence from the document to make a case. • Develop an easy-to-understand retelling.

continued

Figure 2.9 (*continued*)

Step 3: Analyze the Text

What are the big ideas and key details?

[To break down the Gettysburg Address into its big ideas and key details, Robert created the visual organizer below.]

Theme

The United States is, and will continue to be, driven by the ideals of liberty and equality.

Main Idea	**Main Idea**	**Main Idea**
The U.S. was formed on the ideals of liberty and equality, but now those ideals are being tested.	We can never forget the soldiers who fought and died for these ideals.	The nation will survive by remaining committed to these ideals.
Supporting Details	**Supporting Details**	**Supporting Details**
• Eighty-seven years ago (four score and seven), the Founding Fathers brought forth ". . . a new nation, conceived in liberty and dedicated to the proposition that all men are created equal." • "Now we are engaged in a great civil war, testing whether that nation . . . can long endure."	• The soldiers have "consecrated" the battlefield with their bravery. • "The world . . . can never forget what they did here." • "These dead shall not have died in vain."	• "We take increased devotion to that cause." • This nation "shall have a new birth of freedom." • "Government of the people, by the people, for the people, shall not perish from the earth."

Figure 2.9 (*continued*)

Step 4: Decide How You Want Students to Approach the Text

Develop three to seven Reading for Meaning statements.

How do you want students to interact with the text? [Use Figure 2.8 to help you emphasize particular focus skills as you design your statements. For mathematical word problems, see p. 49.]

To help students find main ideas, I'll use these statements:

- Lincoln believes that the soldiers have died in vain.

- Lincoln is convinced that great nations survive challenges.

To help students find main ideas *and* connect the Gettysburg Address to the fundamental U.S. ideals, I'll use this statement:

- Lincoln sees a clear relationship between the past and the present.

To help students understand Lincoln's intent in writing the Gettysburg Address, I'll use these statements:

- A good slogan for the Gettysburg Address would be "We can work it out."

- Lincoln's intent is to make Americans feel guilty about the war.

Are your statements general enough that students can decide whether they agree or disagree before reading? Or would it be better to have students use the statements to make some predictions about the text? Will you be providing the organizer or asking students to create it themselves?

continued

Figure 2.9 (*continued*)

Step 5: Develop Prereading and Post-Reading Questions

Reading for Meaning questions can focus on the content and on students' thinking and reading processes (for example, "How did the statements help you find evidence?" "What reading strategies did you find yourself using?" "How might you use Reading for Meaning on your own?"). For a typical Reading for Meaning lesson, you'll need questions that . . .

- **Stimulate curiosity and activate prior knowledge.**

    As an introductory activity, I'll ask them to tap into what they already know about Abraham Lincoln, the Civil War, and the Gettysburg Address. Then, based on their prior knowledge and statements, I'll ask them to make some predictions about the Gettysburg Address.

- **Deepen reflection and discussion.**

    Questions for thinking about the content include

    - What new insights do you have about the Gettysburg Address? Were your predictions correct?

    - What do you think Lincoln was trying to accomplish by writing it?

    - Why is the Gettysburg Address so famous?

    Questions for thinking about the Reading for Meaning process include

    - How did the Reading for Meaning strategy help you understand and interpret the Gettysburg Address?

    - How might you use Reading for Meaning on your own?

Step 6: Develop a Synthesis Task

How will students apply what they have learned?

I'll have the students create a simple retelling of the Gettysburg Address. To force them to keep their retellings clear and to the point, I'll ask them to create their retellings so that a 3rd grade student could understand them.

Figure 2.10 Sample Planning Form 2: 3rd Grade Mathematics

Step 1: Choose the Text

Select a text, a group of texts, or other information you want students to understand deeply. (Remember: Reading for Meaning lessons can be designed around paintings, lectures, data charts, lab experiments, demonstrations, and many other sources of information.)	Why? How does the text relate to your standards or instructional objectives?
I'm using a word problem for my lesson.	I'm putting a heavy focus on Mathematical Practice 1 from the Common Core State Standards: *Make sense of problems and persevere in solving them*. Word problems are all over the state test. They give kids trouble because the kids have to read carefully and set up the problem themselves, but they want to jump right to the answer without planning. I really want to help them focus on the relevant information and plan their way through the process of finding the hidden question and using it to solve the problem.

Step 2: Clarify the Purpose of the Lesson

Knowledge	Habits of Mind
Students will know • What *relevant information* and *irrelevant information* mean.	Students will develop the habits of • Managing impulsivity. (No leaping to solutions! Plan first.) • Thinking interdependently. • Questioning and posing problems.
Understanding	**Skills**
Students will understand • That not all information in a word problem is equally relevant. • That good problem solving involves careful reading and planning.	Students will be able to • Analyze and solve word problems involving decimals. • Create and solve their own word problems.

continued

Figure 2.10 (*continued*)

Step 3: Analyze the Text

What are the big ideas and key details?

Here's the problem I'll be using: *Most 3rd graders get their hair cut four times a year. Human hair grows at a rate of about 0.5 inches a month. If you get 2 inches of hair cut off during a year, about how much longer will your hair be at the end of that year?*

The irrelevant information is in the first sentence. The second and third sentences contain the relevant information. The hidden question is, "How long does hair grow in a year?" To solve the problem, students need to (1) figure out how much hair grows in a year (6 inches) and (2) subtract 2 inches from the year's growth of 6 inches.

Step 4: Decide How You Want Students to Approach the Text

Develop three to seven Reading for Meaning statements.

How do you want students to interact with the text? [Use Figure 2.8 to help you emphasize particular focus skills as you design your statements. For mathematical word problems, see p. 49.]

To help students separate the relevant from the irrelevant information, I'll use this statement:

- The first sentence contains relevant information.

To help students see the hidden question, I'll use these statements:

- Human hair grows at a rate of 1 inch every 2 months.
- To solve this problem, you need to find out how much hair grows in a year.

To help students think about the problem-solving process, I'll use this statement:

- You need to do only one operation to solve this problem.

Are your statements general enough that students can decide whether they agree or disagree before reading? Or would it be better to have students use the statements to make some predictions about the text? Will you be providing the organizer or asking students to create it themselves?

Figure 2.10 (*continued*)

Step 5: Develop Prereading and Post-Reading Questions

Reading for Meaning questions can focus on the content and on students' thinking and reading processes (for example, "How did the statements help you find evidence?" "What reading strategies did you find yourself using?" "How might you use Reading for Meaning on your own?"). For a typical Reading for Meaning lesson, you'll need questions that . . .

- **Stimulate curiosity and activate prior knowledge**.

  I'll start by having them share their experiences with haircuts. We'll share stories about bad haircuts and about not being able to wait for the hair to grow back. Then I'll connect these experiences to the problem, which is about the rate of hair growth. We'll also talk about relevant versus irrelevant information.

- **Deepen reflection and discussion.**

  I'll ask them these questions:

  - Can you identify the relevant and the irrelevant information? How do you know which is which?

  - What do we mean by a hidden question? What's the hidden question in the problem?

  - Why do good problem solvers also have to be careful readers?

Step 6: Develop a Synthesis Task

How will students apply what they have learned?

I'll let students create their own haircut problems. The problem will have to use at least one decimal. It will also need to include irrelevant information. Students will

- Identify the relevant and the irrelevant information in their problem.

- Identify the hidden question.

- Explain how to solve the problem.

- Solve the problem.

Reading for Meaning Planning Forms

Now you are going to plan a Reading for Meaning lesson for your own classroom. You will be using the content you brought when you started this section to create the lesson. As you work through the planning forms that follow on pages 58–61, refer to the teachers' complete planning forms (Figures 2.9 and 2.10) as models. Remember to keep your students in mind and pay attention to what they will be doing during the different phases of the lesson. Use the poster included with this guide to help students understand their roles in a Reading for Meaning lesson and to help them see how they can use the strategy independently.

Step 1: Choose the Text

Select a text, a group of texts, or other information you want students to understand deeply. (Remember: Reading for Meaning lessons can be designed around paintings, lectures, data charts, lab experiments, demonstrations, and many other sources of information.)	Why? How does the text(s) relate to your standards or instructional objectives?

Step 2: Clarify the Purpose of the Lesson

Knowledge	Habits of Mind
Students will know	Students will develop the habits of
Understanding	**Skills**
Students will understand	Students will be able to

Step 3: Analyze the Text

What are the big ideas and key details?

continued

Step 4: Decide How You Want Students to Approach the Text

Develop three to seven Reading for Meaning statements.

How do you want students to interact with the text? [Use Figure 2.8 to help you emphasize particular focus skills as you design your statements. For mathematical word problems, see p. 49.]

Are your statements general enough that students can decide whether they agree or disagree before reading? Or would it be better to have students use the statements to make some predictions about the text? Will you be providing the organizer or asking students to create it themselves?

Step 5: Develop Prereading and Post-Reading Questions

Reading for Meaning questions can focus on the content and on students' thinking and reading processes (for example, "How did the statements help you find evidence?" "What reading strategies did you find yourself using?" "How might you use Reading for Meaning on your own?"). For a typical Reading for Meaning lesson, you'll need questions that . . .

- **Stimulate curiosity and activate prior knowledge.**

- **Deepen reflection and discussion.**

Step 6: Develop a Synthesis Task

How will students apply what they have learned?

Classroom Tips

In this section, you will find tips for getting the most out of your Reading for Meaning lesson in the classroom.

Introducing Reading for Meaning to Your Students

When you first introduce the strategy, students of all ages—but especially younger students—will need some teacher modeling to see how the process of finding and evaluating evidence works. Using a sample statement and text, use think-alouds (thinking out loud while you go through the evidence-gathering process) to help students hear the kinds of questions they should be asking themselves as they search a text for evidence: Does this information relate to any of the statements? Does it suggest whether the statement is true or false? Is the information black and white, or is it difficult to tell whether the information supports or refutes the statement? Modeling and talking about questions like these help students build both their questioning and their metacognitive habits of minds, which Art Costa and Bena Kallick (2008, 2009) have identified as central to sophisticated thinking in any discipline.

It is also a good idea to discuss *evidence* as a concept and vocabulary term. What is evidence? When, where, and how is evidence used in the world? What does evidence do? When do you use it? What's the difference between an argument that uses evidence and one that doesn't? Whenever a text or a student presents an opinion or takes a position, use it as an opportunity to explore the evidence behind the position. What evidence makes the position strong? Pose simple statements to students, such as "Third grade is much harder than 2nd grade," and ask them to think about the evidence they would use to argue either for or against the statement.

Finally, before using Reading for Meaning in the classroom, explain to students what they will be doing. Use the classroom poster included with this guide to help them internalize their role in the lesson.

Phase One: Introduction of the Text and Topic

Begin with an introductory activity or a question that piques student curiosity and helps students tap into their knowledge and experience. For example, you might start a lesson on reptiles by asking students, "How many of you have ever had a fever? How many of you have spent a long time in a cold pool? What happens to your body when you have a fever? What happens when you spend time in cold water?"

After a brief discussion, help students apply their past knowledge to the learning to come via a bridge: "Fevers and cold pools are two things that can change our body temperatures. But at just about any other time in our lives, our bodies stay at a constant temperature. That's because we're mammals and, as you know, mammals are warm-blooded. But reptiles are cold-blooded. This means they have to spend much of their day warming up and cooling off just to stay alive. And as we'll see in our reading, called 'Cold-Blooded Blues,' this process of trying to keep warm enough without overheating takes an awful lot of work for reptiles."

Introduce several Reading for Meaning statements before the reading and ask students to go over them carefully. Ideally, to increase curiosity and engagement, students should decide whether they agree or disagree with each statement. But sometimes, when statements are text-specific or when students don't have any prior knowledge about the topic of the reading, this process of agreeing or disagreeing amounts to blind guessing. In these cases, you may prefer to have students use the statements to make a few predictions about the text instead.

Phase Two: Active Reading

One way to increase students' abilities to read actively and search for relevant evidence is to teach them how to mark a text using reader's punctuation. A typical set of reader's punctuation looks like this:

S = This information supports a statement.

R = This information refutes a statement.

S/R = This information seems to support *and* refute a statement.

? = This information seems important, but I'm not sure why it's important.

Also, don't forget the power of reading aloud, especially—but not only—with younger students and struggling readers. Reading aloud relieves students of the stress they may experience during reading and allows them to focus their attention specifically on the evidence in the text. Reading aloud enables you to inflect your voice to help students key in on specific parts of the text, and it allows you to pause at particular points in the text to open discussion about whether what you just read supports or refutes a specific statement. As you read aloud, you can collect evidence on an easel or on the board using a large Reading for Meaning organizer (see Figure 2.11).

Figure 2.11   Reading for Meaning Organizer for a Lesson on Reptiles

Evidence For	Statements	Evidence Against
	A reptile's body temperature is the same as the temperature of the surrounding environment.	
	There are probably more reptiles in Kansas than in Canada.	
	Reptiles can be more patient than mammals.	

While students read silently and collect evidence on their organizers, take the opportunity to conduct formative assessment of students' comprehension. Are they collecting relevant evidence? Are particular statements giving the class difficulty?

Phase Three: Reflection and Discussion

After students have completed the reading and collected evidence, give them 5 to 10 minutes to discuss their ideas in small groups. Small-group settings help students practice two of Costa and Kallick's (2008, 2009) critical habits of mind: thinking interdependently and listening with understanding and empathy. Small groups also enable students to test and refine their ideas before the larger discussion. In their groups, students should go through the statements one by one and discuss their takes on each statement and the evidence they collected in support or refutation of each statement. Remind students that disagreement is natural and should not be avoided; however, all opinions need to be treated with respect. When groups cannot come to collective agreement on a particular statement, encourage them to tweak or rewrite the statement so that everyone can agree (or disagree) with it.

Group discussion gives you further opportunities to conduct some real-time formative assessment. Listen in on group discussions. When groups are struggling to reach agreement, step in to serve as a comprehension coach. Help groups pinpoint sources of confusion or differences by first figuring out what they do agree on.

Complete the phase with a whole-class discussion. Use this discussion time to help students reflect on the content (what they learned from the text) and the process (what they learned about themselves as readers). Use questions to guide reflection and discussion. Content-related questions sound like this:

- How have your ideas about reptiles and cold-bloodedness changed as a result of the reading?

- Is cold-bloodedness a clear disadvantage? Are there any ways it can be considered an advantage?

- What would the ideal habitat for a reptile be like?

Process-related questions sound like this:

- How did the statements help you read with greater purpose?

- Which reading and thinking techniques did we use before, during, and after reading? How did they help?

- Can you apply any of these techniques to your own reading? How?

Remember: the ultimate goal of Reading for Meaning is to help students increase their power as readers by teaching them how to apply the comprehension skills that are embedded in the strategy. As you use Reading for Meaning with greater frequency, make sure you engage students in metacognitive reflection, or "thinking about thinking." Review with students the strategies they used . . .

- *Before reading:* Activate prior knowledge, make predictions, establish purpose.

- *During reading:* Read actively, search for relevant information and evidence, make notes.

- *After reading:* Look back on learning, discuss and refine thinking, shore up gaps in comprehension, apply learning.

Explain to students that these are the skills that separate great readers from average readers, and encourage them to use these skills and strategies independently.

Phase Four: Synthesis

One of the simplest and most effective ways to have students synthesize their learning is to use a Reading for Meaning statement as the basis of a persuasive essay. The statement can come from the lesson, or you can introduce a new one. Either way, the statement should be one that sits at the center of the content, ties back to your instructional objectives, and requires students to draw heavily on the texts to make their case (for example, "Cold-bloodedness makes daily life difficult for reptiles").

A great tool to help students plan and structure persuasive essays is a 3 x 3 Writing Frame. A 3 x 3 Writing Frame makes clear to students what the beginning, middle, and end of their persuasive essays need to contain. It also helps students communicate their ideas with the kind of clarity and precision that are the mark of careful thinkers. Figure 2.12 shows an elementary school student's 3 x 3 Writing Frame for a persuasive essay that responds to the statement "Cold-bloodedness makes daily life difficult for reptiles."

Figure 2.12 Elementary-Level 3 x 3 Writing Frame (Persuasive Essay)

BEGINNING What are you trying to prove?	MIDDLE What is your evidence? Prove it.		END Close the writing.
Make your case or restate the question.	List three reasons.	Elaborate on each reason (or provide an example).	Wrap it up.
Cold-bloodedness makes daily life difficult for reptiles.	• Must shuttle back and forth between sun and shade. • If the sun is too hot, a reptile will behave strangely or even die. • As body temperature drops, so does performance.	Must bask in the sun to warm up before chasing prey in the shade. Can't pant or sweat to cool off like mammals so it has to be careful not to overheat. When body temperature drops by 18°F, a reptile's running speed is half and digestion takes twice as long.	Because they are cold-blooded, reptiles have to spend a lot of their energy warming up and cooling down. How would you like it if you had to worry all day about your body temperature?

Younger students can be introduced to persuasive writing using statements as well. With younger students, teachers sometimes refer to persuasive essays as "I Think" essays. The first sentence of an "I Think" essay always tells what the student thinks about the statement (for example, "I think bats are more helpful than harmful").

Of course, there are many other kinds of tasks you can use to help students synthesize and demonstrate their learning. Throughout this guide, you'll find teachers who designed tasks asking students to

- Speculate on Chekhov's intent in writing "A Nincompoop" (p. 29).

- Create a balanced meal (p. 37).

- Create their own mathematical word problems (p. 39).

- Develop a retelling of the Gettysburg Address that a 3rd grader would understand (p. 40).

- Choose the graph that best explains the behavior of a pendulum and defend their choice (p. 43).

THOUGHTWORK

Before the Next Section

Between this section and the next, you should teach your Reading for Meaning lesson in your own classroom. Use the questions below to help you identify problems you might encounter as you use Reading for Meaning in your classroom and to develop solutions to potential problems before they occur.

Activity: Rooting Out Problems

1. What types of problems might you encounter while teaching a Reading for Meaning lesson?

2. What patterns do you see as you think about these potential problems?

3. Select one type of problem. What are the facts you know about this problem?

4. What are some possible causes for this type of problem?

5. What is the best solution to this problem?

THOUGHTWORK

When it comes to improving the quality of instruction, there are few resources more valuable than a critical friend who listens to your thinking, observes your work, and offers constructive feedback to help you get better results in the classroom. That's why we strongly recommend that you select a critical friend and schedule time to observe each other in the classroom. The two of you should take turns: you present your lesson to your class while your partner takes notes. Then switch roles. Use the following observation guide to structure your observation notes. When you start Section 3, be prepared to share what you have learned as a result of implementing and observing a Reading for Meaning lesson.

Reading for Meaning Observation Guide

Introduction of the Text and Topic

1. How did the teacher stimulate students' interest or curiosity?

2. How did the teacher activate students' prior knowledge?

3. Did the teacher clearly connect the introductory activity to the topic or text?   ☐ Yes   ☐ No
Comments:

4. Did the introductory activity establish a strong purpose for reading?   ☐ Yes   ☐ No
Comments:

5. Were students able to use the statements to formulate initial responses or make predictions?   ☐ Yes   ☐ No
Comments:

THOUGHTWORK

Reading for Meaning Observation Guide (*continued*)

Active Reading

1. How actively engaged were students while they read?

2. How well did students collect evidence to support and/or refute the statements?

Reflection and Discussion

1. How well did students discuss the Reading for Meaning statements, their responses, and the evidence they collected . . .

- In small groups?

- During whole-class discussion?

Synthesis

1. What task did the teacher assign to help students synthesize their learning?

2. How effectively did students apply what they learned to the task?

Evaluating the Lesson

The goal in this section is to deepen your understanding of Reading for Meaning by working in teams to reflect on the strategy and refine your use of it in the classroom.

In this section you will

■ Share your experiences implementing and observing a Reading for Meaning lesson in the classroom.

■ Reflect more deeply on your own lesson by exploring specific questions related to each of the four phases of Reading for Meaning.

Sharing Your Experience

Now that you have presented a lesson using Reading for Meaning and observed one of your peers doing the same, it's time to share what you have learned with your learning club. We recommend following the steps below:

Step 1: Using the observation guide provided in Section 2's ThoughtWork (pp. 68–69), present your observations of *your partner's* lesson to the group.

Step 2: When you are finished, your partner will comment on the challenges and successes he or she experienced while presenting his or her lesson.

Step 3: Next, switch roles so that your partner can present his or her observations of *your* lesson.

Step 4: Now it's your turn to share the challenges and successes you experienced with your own lesson.

Consider the following questions when you share your thoughts on your own lesson.

Activity: Reflecting on Your Reading for Meaning Lesson

1. What goal(s) did you set out to achieve?

2. What steps did you take? What was hard for you?

3. What came naturally?

4. What worked about the lesson, and what just wouldn't work?

After the presentations to the group, meet again with your partner to discuss the notes you both made. What stood out in your partner's lesson? What questions did the lesson raise for you about the strategy? How might you improve on your partner's lesson or on the process of implementing Reading for Meaning in general?

Now consider the feedback your partner gave you. Use the space below to expand on your partner's ideas for how to improve your lesson. Include what you thought you did well, how your students responded to the lesson, what aspects of the process worked best for you, and what you might do differently next time.

Activity: Improving Your Use of Reading for Meaning

How might you improve your next lesson? How might you improve your implementation of Reading for Meaning?

For the ThoughtWork activity on the next page, you will design a second Reading for Meaning lesson for your classroom. You may choose to begin planning now as part of a learning club meeting, or you may prefer to plan on your own or with your critical friend outside the meeting.

ThoughtWork

Before the Next Section

Before the final section, complete the following exercises:

- Plan another lesson using the Reading for Meaning strategy. Use the planning forms provided on pages 58–61 to guide you.

- Present the lesson to your students.

- Collect three samples of student work from your lesson and bring them to the next meeting. The student work you collect should reflect what you believe to be three distinct skill levels: low, average, and high. To see how one teacher selected her levels, preview pages 76–82 in Section 4.

- Bring enough copies of your student work to distribute to the members of your learning club.

Learning from Student Work

The goal in this section is to examine student work at various levels of proficiency and use it to help you refine your work in designing and delivering Reading for Meaning lessons.

In this section you will

■ See how a teacher selected and analyzed her three samples of student work.

■ Share and discuss the student work you collected from the last section.

■ Develop a rubric for assessing student work based on your discussion and samples.

■ Plan your next steps in building students' reading, thinking, and comprehension skills.

Examining Samples

In this final section, you are going to use student work to assess the effectiveness of your instruction, your students' reading and thinking skills, and your students' grasp of the content. Let's start with a model to guide your examination of the student work you collected for this section.

Here is a synthesis task designed by a 7th grade teacher. Notice how the task has students use the Reading for Meaning process of responding to the statement, taking a position, and collecting evidence.

Sample Synthesis Task: "The Road Not Taken"

In our lives we all need to make choices. For various reasons, some are made quickly, while others may require much consideration. Think of a decision you've made recently that has caused you some happiness or regret. Did you think about the possible effects of your decision before making it?

Today, we are going to read Robert Frost's poem "The Road Not Taken." In this poem, Frost weighs the pros and cons of choosing a path when confronted with a fork in the road. As you read, you will need to collect evidence to help argue either for or against this statement: *The poet is unhappy with his choice.* Use the organizer to help you collect evidence and make inferences to argue your position. After you gather your evidence, you will use it to write a brief thesis (persuasive essay) defending your position. In your essay, you will discuss whether the poet was pleased or unhappy with his choice and explain how you know using evidence from the poem.

Now let's look at three students' responses to this task at three levels of proficiency: low, average, and high. For each work sample, we have included both the student's completed organizer and his or her essay.

Low-Level Example of Student Work

Organizer

Evidence For (Agree)	Statement	Evidence Against (Disagree)
	The poet is unhappy with his choice.	"Then took the other, as just as fair" —If they are both fair, why would he be unhappy? "I took the one less traveled by, and that has made all the difference" —He is proud he took a chance. I bet he feels good.

Essay

I disagree that the poet is unhappy with his choice. The poet said he took a road that was just as fair. Being fair is important and should make you feel okay with your choice, even if it took a long time to make it. I also think he was proud of himself by taking the road most of the other people didn't. He said his choice made a difference and making a difference in the world or even just your own life is good. So why would someone be unhappy if they took a road that was fair and made a difference? It isn't like he cheated or took something from someone. He shouldn't be unhappy with his choice and I don't think he is.

Average Example of Student Work

Organizer

Evidence For (Agree)	Statement	Evidence Against (Disagree)
"And sorry I could not travel both" —If he was happy, he wouldn't be sorry. "Oh, I kept the first for another day! . . . I doubted if I should ever come back." —He tried to tell himself he could come back, but figures out he probably won't and that can make you unhappy, it's like he can see his life passing him by.	The poet is unhappy with his choice.	Then took the other, as just as fair, And having perhaps the better claim" —He tries to tell himself he made the right choice.

Essay

In Robert Frost's poem, "The Road Not Taken," the poet is unhappy overall with his choice. At times, he tries to make himself feel better about his difficult choice, but in the end, he did not feel good about the choice he made. First of all, the poet states, "And sorry I could not travel both." When people say they are sorry about not being able to do something, that is a feeling of regret. If the poet felt good about his choice, he wouldn't say he was sorry, he probably would have said he was confident or pleased.

On the other hand, when he says, "Then took the other, as just as fair, and having perhaps the better claim" I think he is trying to make himself feel better about making his choice. Having a better claim sounds good, but he still isn't sure which road is a better choice. I know when I feel good about my choices I am strong about them. But the poet doesn't seem strong or confident about his choice. Even though the poet might not be completely unhappy, there seems to be an overall sad tone to the poem.

Finally, Frost wrote, "Oh I kept the first for another day! . . . I doubted if I should ever come back." You can tell he isn't happy about not being able to come back to try the other road another time. If the author was happy, he wouldn't have so many doubts or be sorry for his choice.

continued

High-Level Example of Student Work

Organizer

Evidence For (Agree)	Statement	Evidence Against (Disagree)
"And sorry I could not travel both" —He has regrets. "And be one traveler, long I stood" —Gives a lonely and sad picture of someone who wishes for help. "I shall be telling this with a sigh/ Somewhere ages and ages hence" —If he had been happy with his choice, he wouldn't imagine retelling this choice with a sigh, probably with a smile. "I doubted if I should ever come back." —He thinks about the future and "Yet knowing how way leads on to way," realizes he probably won't ever be back to try the other road. —I think he would have felt better if he didn't have to make a decision.	The poet is unhappy with his choice.	"Because it was grassy and wanted wear; . . . Had worn them really about the same" —He tries to find a reason to take one over the other, but can't come up with a real reason. "I took the one less traveled by, And that has made all the difference." —Seems like he is trying to give himself something to feel good about.

Essay

In Robert Frost's poem, "The Road Not Taken," the poet is unhappy with the whole idea of having to make a choice. Throughout the poem, Frost seems doubtful, lonely, and full of regret. He expresses almost no happiness or confidence. After much uncertainty, he ends the poem with a hint of optimism; yet despite his effort, the overall tone of the poem is clearly not one of happiness.

Within the poem, there is evidence that Frost is sorrowful and even willing to fool himself in order to feel better. In just the second line, he admits, "And sorry I could not travel both" when he was confronted with the fork in the road. He later tries to convince himself one choice might be better than the other when he says, "Because it was grassy and wanted wear." But then he admits that the paths "Had worn them really about the same." Here the poet reveals that his notion that the grass "wanted wear" was really just wishful thinking. He resorts to lying to himself in an effort to make himself feel better.

Throughout the poem, Frost gives the reader the feeling he is lonely. He talks about how he is "one traveler" who stood for a long time in front of the two roads, trying to make his decision. This retelling portion looks back on the memory in an unpleasant way, not a way someone who felt happy about a choice would describe it. The image of a traveler standing alone in the woods creates an empty feeling.

Another strong feeling in the poem is regret. "Yet knowing how way leads on to way, I doubted if I should ever come back" is a very strong example of the poet realizing that time will pass and that he will never get the chance to travel "The Road Not Taken." Furthermore, he does not express confidence in his decision making. Instead, Frost ends the poem with, "I shall be telling this with a sigh/Somewhere ages and ages hence." Even as he is writing the poem, he predicts he will not look back at his choice with happiness but with a sigh of regret.

Overall, I think this is a depressing poem. Frost takes us through his decision-making process, which is filled with doubts and sorrow. In the final lines of the poem, Frost writes, "I took the one less traveled by, And that has made all the difference." Some people might read that line as an expression of pride, but I think at the last minute, he is trying to convince himself he traveled an adventurous road, so he can perhaps feel better about his choice when he is older. If this poem were being told by someone who was truly happy with his choice, the mood would have been much different. Perhaps it would have been titled, "The Road Taken."

Take a moment to examine your thinking about the student work samples you have just reviewed. What do you notice about the high-level sample that is missing from the other two? Which criteria might you use to compare these levels, and how might you describe each sample based on those criteria? Record your thoughts on page 80.

Activity: Reflecting on Sample Student Work

Possible criteria:

The teacher who developed the essay task on "The Road Not Taken" created the rubric in Figure 4.1 to guide her assessment of student work. You may want to use this rubric as a model when you develop your own rubric later in this section.

Figure 4.1   Teacher's Rubric for "The Road Not Taken" Essay

	High-Level Performance	Average Performance	Low-Level or Struggling Performance
Content	• Contains a strong, well-developed thesis statement. • Uses at least three quotes from the text in a meaningful way to support the thesis. • Writing is focused on the topic. • Includes and responds to a possible counterargument to the thesis.	• Contains a good thesis statement. • Uses some quotes from the text to support the thesis. • Writing is focused on the topic for the majority of the piece. • Touches on a counterargument to the thesis.	• Contains a weak or no thesis statement. • Uses few or no quotes from the text to support the thesis. • Includes limited and/or irrelevant/off-topic information. • Makes no mention of a counterargument to the thesis.
Process	• The organizer is used to gather quotes from the text and analyze the poet's writing and thoughts.	• The organizer is used to gather some quotes from the text and make comments on possible meanings.	• The organizer contains minimal information and little to no commentary or analysis.
Product	• Contains a strong introduction and conclusion. • Consistently uses strong and varied sentence structure. • Demonstrates sophisticated use of transitions. • Follows conventions of standard written English and contains few errors.	• Contains a solid introduction and conclusion. • Uses a variety of sentences. • Demonstrates some use of transitions. • Contains no glaring errors in grammar, spelling, or mechanics.	• Contains a weak introduction and/or conclusion. • Sentences tend to be simple or poorly developed. • Demonstrates limited use or total lack of transitions. • Shows no signs of having been proofread to root out errors.

Let's now turn to your thought process in selecting your own student work samples. Take a few minutes to reexamine your samples, keeping in mind the following questions:

- How did you select work from each level?

- What criteria did you use to choose this work?

Record your thoughts in the space provided below.

Activity: How You Selected Student Work Samples

Level One: Expert

Level Two: Proficient

Level Three: Apprentice

Next, meet with your partner to share the student work you collected. Work together to analyze the content, process, and product of the student work. Keep in mind that examining this student work is less about whether commas and semicolons are in the right place and more about how well your students have put their understanding of the content and the strategic reading process to work.

Note that we provided two different formats for this collaborative analysis. Option 1 uses questions to guide the analysis. Option 2 uses a rubric format. Decide which option works better for you and your partner and use it to conduct your analysis.

Activity: Analyzing Student Work, Option 1—Questions

Content

1. What does the student work suggest about students' grasp of the key ideas and details?

2. Which parts of the content are firmly in their grasp?

3. Which ideas and details are slipping through the cracks?

Process

1. What does this work suggest about how your students use textual evidence to justify their ideas?

Product

1. What similarities and differences do you notice in the quality of student work?

2. How well are students communicating their ideas?

3. What signs are there that students are reaching toward excellence? What patterns of strength and weakness do you find compelling?

Activity: Analyzing Student Work, Option 2—Rubric

	High-Level Performance	Average Performance	Low-Level or Struggling Performance
Content			
Process			
Product			

Now, summarize what you have learned from your analysis and plan your next steps.

Activity: Thinking About the Next Steps

Content

What have you learned about your students' grasp of ideas and details in the content area?

Process

What have you learned about your students' ability to find evidence and use it to justify claims?

Product

What have you learned about your students' ability to communicate? What motivates them to reach toward excellence?

Interventions

How will you use these insights? What kinds of instructional interventions do you need to make?*

*For a collection of ready-to-use instructional techniques for helping students meet your benchmarks, see *Tools for Promoting Active, In-Depth Learning* (Silver, Strong, & Perini, 2001).

Where Am I Now?

Before completing this guide, take a few minutes to think about your own grasp of the Reading for Meaning strategy. Looking at the strategy implementation milestones below, where do you think you are now? What do you need to do to move to the next level?

Strategy Implementation Milestones

✓ I know what Reading for Meaning is and can describe what it looks like in the classroom.

✓ I understand Reading for Meaning and can explain how it works.

✓ I have planned several Reading for Meaning lessons, used them in my classroom, and reflected with my colleagues on their effects on my students.

✓ My students have a solid understanding of Reading for Meaning, and I can see them transferring the thinking skills involved in the strategy to other situations.

✓ I am ready to teach other people how to use Reading for Meaning.

Appendix: What Are the Habits of Mind?

Habits of mind are dispositions that are skillfully and mindfully employed by characteristically intelligent, successful people when they are confronted with problems whose solutions are not immediately apparent.

The habits of mind as identified by Art Costa and Bena Kallick (2008, 2009) are

- Persisting.

- Thinking and communicating with clarity and precision.

- Managing impulsivity.

- Gathering data through all senses.

- Listening with understanding and empathy.

- Creating, imagining, and innovating.

- Thinking flexibly.

- Responding with wonderment and awe.

- Thinking about thinking (metacognition).

- Taking responsible risks.

- Striving for accuracy.

- Finding humor.

- Questioning and posing problems.

- Thinking interdependently.

- Applying past knowledge to new situations.

- Remaining open to continuous learning.

To learn more about the habits of mind and how schools across the globe are using them to improve teaching and learning, go to www.instituteforhabitsofmind.com.

References

Chekhov, A. (1960). A nincompoop. In A. Dunnigan (Trans.), *Anton Chekhov: Selected stories* (pp. 20–22). New York: Signet Classic.

Costa, A. L., & Kallick, B. (2008). *Learning and leading with habits of mind: 16 essential characteristics for success*. Alexandria, VA: ASCD.

Costa, A. L., & Kallick, B. (2009). *Habits of mind across the curriculum: Practical and creative strategies for teachers*. Alexandria, VA: ASCD.

Dickinson, E. (2004). There's a certain slant of light. In H. Bloom (Ed.), *The best poems of the English language* (pp. 579–580). New York: HarperCollins.

Du Bois, W. E. B. (1989). *The souls of black folk*. New York: Bantam.

Durkin, D. (1978–1979). What classroom observation reveals about reading comprehension instruction. *Reading Research Quarterly, 14,* 481–533.

Frost, R. (1969). The road not taken. In E. C. Lathem (Ed.), *The poetry of Robert Frost* (p. 105). New York: Henry Holt and Company.

Hamilton, A. (2003). No. 30: Concerning the general power of taxation. In C. Rossiter (Ed.), *The Federalist papers* (pp. 183–188). New York: Signet Classic.

Herber, H. (1978). *Teaching reading in the content areas* (2nd ed.). Englewood Cliffs, NJ: Prentice-Hall.

Joyce, B. R., & Showers, B. (2002). *Student achievement through staff development* (3rd ed.). Alexandria, VA: ASCD.

Keene, E. O. (2010). New horizons in comprehension. *Educational Leadership, 67*(6), 69–73.

Keene, E. O., & Zimmermann, S. (2007). *Mosaic of thought: The power of comprehension strategy instruction* (2nd ed.). Portsmouth, NH: Heinemann.

Pressley, M. (2006). *Reading instruction that works: The case for balanced teaching*. New York: Guilford Press.

Pressley, M., & Afflerbach, P. (1995). *Verbal protocols of reading: The nature of constructively responsive reading*. Hillsdale, NJ: Lawrence Erlbaum.

Schmoker, M. (2005). Here and now: Improving teaching and learning. In R. DuFour, R. Eaker, & R. DuFour (Eds.), *On common ground: The power of professional learning communities* (pp. xi–xvi). Bloomington, IN: Solution Tree.

Silver, H. F., & Perini, M. J. (2010). *Classroom curriculum design: How strategic units improve instruction and engage students in meaningful learning.* Ho-Ho-Kus, NJ: Thoughtful Education Press.

Silver, H. F., Strong, R. W., & Perini, M. J. (2001). *Tools for promoting active, in-depth learning* (2nd ed.). Ho-Ho-Kus, NJ: Thoughtful Education Press.

Silver, H. F., Strong, R. W., & Perini, M. J. (2007). *The strategic teacher: Selecting the right research-based strategy for every lesson.* Alexandria, VA: ASCD.

Wyatt, D., Pressley, M., El-Dinary, P. B., Stein, S., Evans, P., & Brown, R. (1993). Comprehension strategies, worth and credibility monitoring, and evaluations: Cold and hot cognition when experts read professional articles that are important to them. *Learning and Individual Differences, 5,* 49–72.

Zimmermann, S., & Hutchins, C. (2003). *7 keys to comprehension.* New York: Three Rivers Press.

About the Authors

Harvey F. Silver, EdD, is president of Silver Strong & Associates and Thoughtful Education Press. He has conducted numerous workshops for school districts and state education departments throughout the United States. He was the principal consultant for the Georgia Critical Thinking Skills Program and the Kentucky Thoughtful Education Teacher Leadership Program. With the late Richard W. Strong, he developed The Thoughtful Classroom, a renowned professional development initiative dedicated to the goal of "Making Students as Important as Standards." Dr. Silver may be reached at Silver Strong & Associates, 227 First Street, Ho-Ho-Kus, NJ 07423; 1-800-962-4432; hsilver@thoughtfulclassroom.com.

Susan C. Morris, a former classroom teacher, has over two decades of experience developing practical applications for teachers, students, and parents in the areas of learning styles, multiple intelligences, brain-based research, experiential learning, and curriculum design. As a consultant and coach, she uses a train-the-trainer approach to foster sustainable professional development and incorporate technology to enhance and promote continuous professional learning. She may be reached at smorris@thoughtfulclassroom.com.

Victor Klein, an experienced educator and former building administrator, has been a trainer for Silver Strong & Associates during the last 25 years. He has supervised three Thoughtful Classroom schools at the primary, secondary, and middle school levels. As a trainer, his areas of professional development expertise lie in professional learning communities, teacher rounds, administrative training, and unit and lesson design. He may be reached at vklein@thoughtfulclassroom.com.